ITIL® 4 Foundation
Courseware - English

Colophon

Title:	ITIL® 4 Foundation Courseware - English
Authors:	Van Haren Learning Solutions A.O.
Publisher:	Van Haren Publishing, 's-Hertogenbosch
ISBN Hard Copy:	978 94 018 0393 9
Edition:	First edition, first print, February 28th, 2019 Revised edition, first print, February 2020 Revised edition, second print, July 2021
Design:	Van Haren Publishing, 's-Hertogenbosch
Copyright:	© Van Haren Publishing 2021

For further information about Van Haren Publishing please e-mail us at: info@vanharen.net or visit our website: www.vanharen.net

This material contains diagrams and text Information based upon: AXELOS ITIL® material. Material is reproduced under licence from AXELOS All rights reserved.

No part of this publication may be reproduced in any form by print, photo print, microfilm or any other means without written permission by the publisher.
Although this publication has been composed with much care, neither author, nor editor, nor publisher can accept any liability for damage caused by possible errors and/or incompleteness in this publication.

Material in this document has been sourced from ITIL® Service Operation 2011 edition. No part of this document may be reproduced in any form without the written permission of both Van Haren Publishing and AXELOS Limited. Permission can be requested at info@vanharen.net and licensing@AXELOS.com.

Publisher about the Courseware

The Courseware was created by experts from the industry who served as the author(s) for this publication. The input for the material is based on existing publications and the experience and expertise of the author(s). The material has been revised by trainers who also have experience working with the material. Close attention was also paid to the key learning points to ensure what needs to be mastered.

The objective of the courseware is to provide maximum support to the trainer and to the student, during his or her training. The material has a modular structure and according to the author(s) has the highest success rate should the student opt for examination. The Courseware is also accredited for this reason, wherever applicable.

In order to satisfy the requirements for accreditation the material must meet certain quality standards. The structure, the use of certain terms, diagrams and references are all part of this accreditation. Additionally, the material must be made available to each student in order to obtain full accreditation. To optimally support the trainer and the participant of the training assignments, practice exams and results are provided with the material.

Direct reference to advised literature is also regularly covered in the sheets so that students can find additional information concerning a particular topic. The decision to leave out notes pages from the Courseware was to encourage students to take notes throughout the material.

Although the courseware is complete, the possibility that the trainer deviates from the structure of the sheets or chooses to not refer to all the sheets or commands does exist. The student always has the possibility to cover these topics and go through them on their own time. It is recommended to follow the structure of the courseware and publications for maximum exam preparation.

The courseware and the recommended literature are the perfect combination to learn and understand the theory.

-- Van Haren Publishing

Other publications by Van Haren Publishing

Van Haren Publishing (VHP) specializes in titles on Best Practices, methods and standards within four domains:
- IT and IT Management
- Architecture (Enterprise and IT)
- Business Management and
- Project Management

Van Haren Publishing is also publishing on behalf of leading organizations and companies: ASLBiSL Foundation, BRMI, CA, Centre Henri Tudor, Gaming Works, IACCM, IAOP, IFDC, Innovation Value Institute, IPMA-NL, ITSqc, NAF, KNVI, PMI-NL, PON, The Open Group, The SOX Institute.

Topics are (per domain):

IT and IT Management	Enterprise Architecture	Project Management
ABC of ICT	ArchiMate®	A4-Projectmanagement
ASL®	GEA®	DSDM/Atern
CATS CM®	Novius Architectuur Methode	ICB / NCB
CMMI®		ISO 21500
COBIT®	TOGAF®	MINCE®
e-CF		M_o_R®
ISO/IEC 20000	**Business Management**	MSP®
ISO/IEC 27001/27002	*BABOK® Guide*	P3O®
ISPL	BiSL® and BiSL® Next	*PMBOK® Guide*
IT4IT®	BRMBOK™	Praxis®
IT-CMF™	BTF	PRINCE2®
IT Service CMM	EFQM	
ITIL®	eSCM	
MOF	IACCM	
MSF	ISA-95	
SABSA	ISO 9000/9001	
SAF	OPBOK	
SIAM™	SixSigma	
TRIM	SOX	
VeriSM™	SqEME®	

For the latest information on VHP publications, visit our website: www.vanharen.net.

Table of content

	Slide number	Page number
Reflection		7
Agenda		9
Introduction	(1)	11
Key Concepts of Service Management	(10)	15
Services and products	(13)	16
Value and value co-creation	(15)	17
Organizations, providers, consumers, and other stakeholders	(16)	18
Service relationships	(19)	19
Value: outcomes, costs, and risks	(21)	20
Summary & Practice Questions	(25)	22
The four dimensions of service management	(32)	25
Organizations and people	(34)	26
Information and technology	(35)	27
Partners and suppliers	(41)	30
Value streams and processes	(44)	31
External factors	(47)	33
Summary & Practice Questions	(48)	33
The ITIL service value system	(53)	35
Service value system overview	(65)	41
The ITIL guiding principles	(69)	43
Summary & Practice Questions	(77)	47
ITIL guiding principles	(83)	49
Focus on Value	(93)	54
Start where you are	(97)	56
Progress iteratively	(101)	58
Collaborate	(105)	60
Optimize and automate	(118)	67
Summary & Practice Questions	(122)	69

Service management practices	(129)	72
ITIL management practices	(130)	72
Summary & Practice Questions	(168)	91
General and Technical management practices	(175)	94
Summary & Practice Questions	(190)	102

Exercises

1. Service management key concepts	107
2. ITIL key concepts	111
3. ITIL practices	114
4. Case Value Streams	119
Sample paper 1	121
Sample paper 1 Answers and Rationale	132
Sample paper 2	151
Sample paper 1 Answers and Rationale	162
Syllabus	180
Glossary	188
Literature mapping with ITIL 4 Foundation Pocketguide	198

Self-Reflection of understanding Diagram

'What you do not measure, you cannot control.' – Tom Peters

Fill in this diagram to self-evaluate your understanding of the material. This is an evaluation of how well you know the material and how well you understand it. In order to pass the exam successfully you should be aiming to reach the higher end of Level 3. If you really want to become a pro, then you should be aiming for Level 4. Your overall level of understanding will naturally follow the learning curve. So, it's important to keep track of where you are at each point of the training and address any areas of difficulty.

Based on where you are within the Self-Reflection of Understanding diagram you can evaluate the progress of your own training.

Level of Understanding	Before Training (Pre-knowledge)	Training Part 1 (1st Half)	Training Part 2 (2nd Half)	After studying / reading the book	After exercises and the Practice exam
Level 4 I can explain the content and apply it.					
Level 3 I get it! I am right where I am supposed to be.					Ready for the exam!
Level 2 I almost have it but could use more practice.					
Level 1 I am learning but don't quite get it yet.					

(Self-Reflection of Understanding Diagram)

Write down the problem areas that you are still having difficulty with so that you can consolidate them yourself, or with your trainer. After you have had a look at these, then you should evaluate to see if you now have a better understanding of where you actually are on the learning curve.

Troubleshooting

	Problem areas:	*Topic:*
Part 1		
Part 2		
You have gone through the book and studied.		
You have answered the questions and done the practice exam.		

Timetable

	Day 1, Key concepts of service management
Part 1	Introduction
	Value creation, outcomes, costs and risks
	Services and service relationships
	The four dimensions
	Lunch
Part 2	The ITIL service value system
	The activities of the service value chain
	The nature and use of the guiding principles

	Day 2, Selected ITIL practices and key terms
Part 1	Service management practices
	Lunch
	Service management practices (continued)
	General practices
Part 2	Technical practices
	Set up exam
	ITIL® Exam

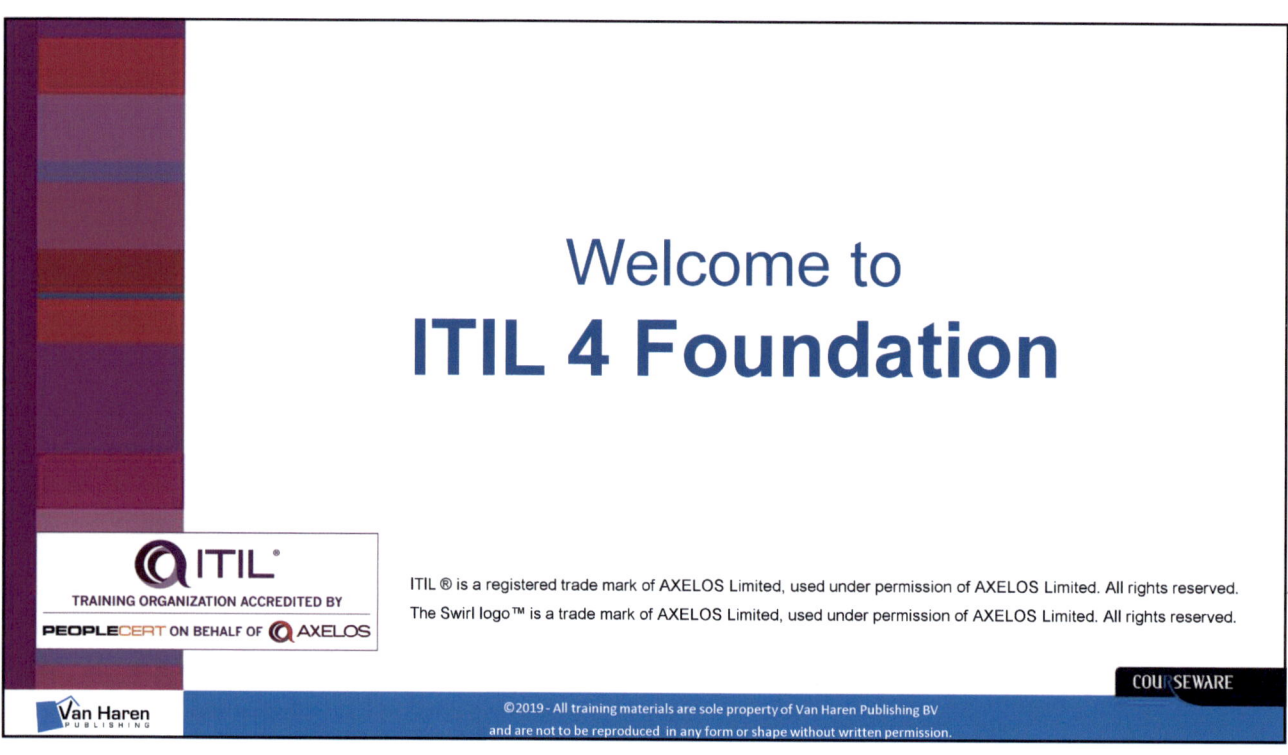

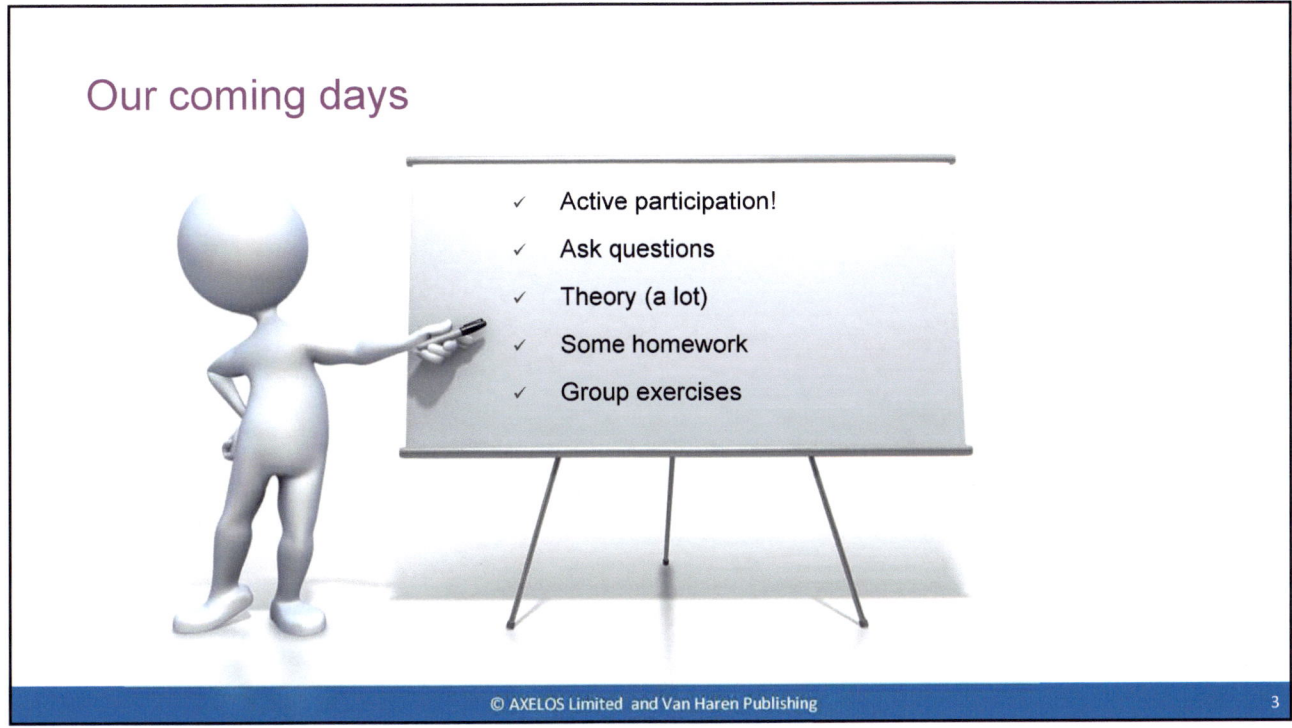
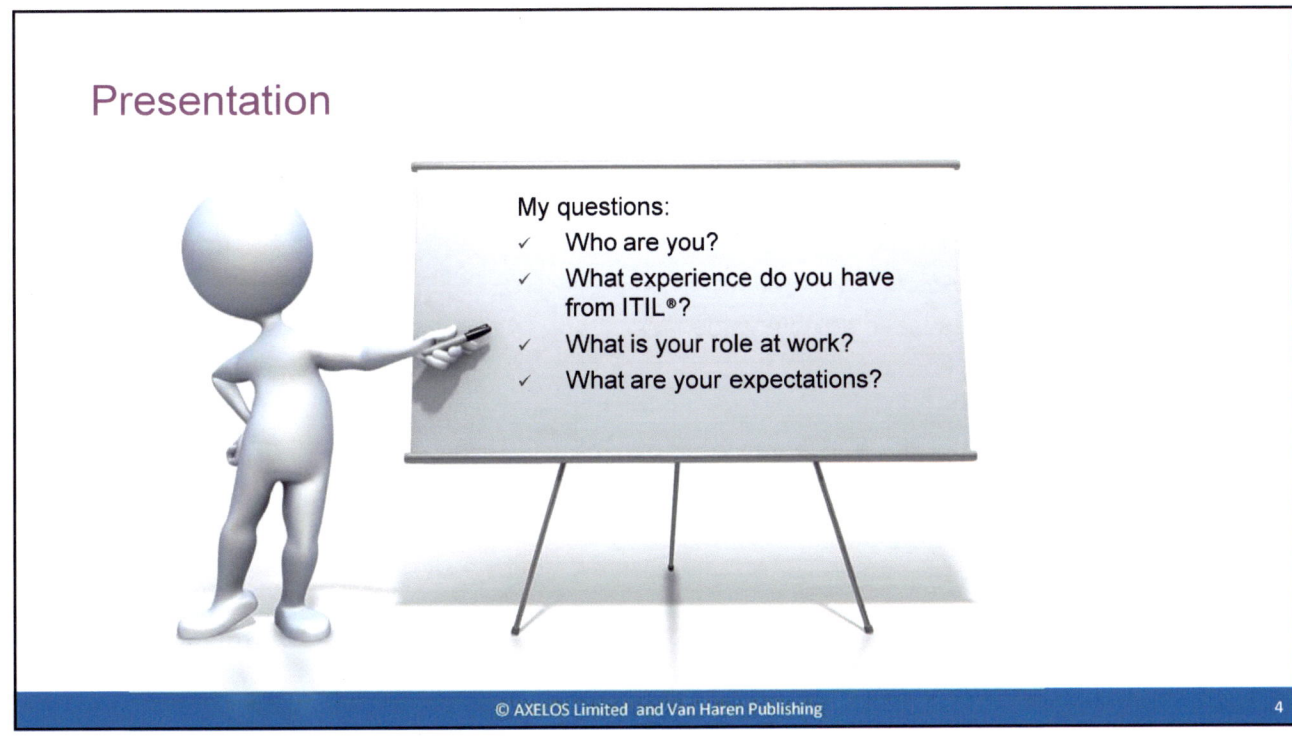

Course schedule
- Day 1: Key concepts of service management
  - Value creation, outcomes, costs and risks
  - Services and service relationships
  - The four dimensions
  - The ITIL service value system
  - The activities of the service value chain
  - The nature and use of the guiding principles
- Day 2: Selected ITIL practices and key terms
  - Service management practices
  - General practices
  - Technical practices

ITIL is evolving…

- ✓ From process focus to holistic view
- ✓ From fragmented lifecycle to end-to-end
- ✓ From major releases to continual improvement
- ✓ From operational silos to flexible value flow

Since the latest update of ITIL in 2011 we have seen huge changes impacting most organizations who have adopted ITIL best practices. There is a clear need to adapt to changes in markets, technologies and ways of working and ITIL is no exception.

Background to ITIL 4

Principles as a central theme

There has been a clear trend among the commonly used frameworks, models and methodologies to move away from rules and focus more on principles.

We see this development as a positive thing in general as it can make interoperability and integration between frameworks and methodologies more accepted as most basic underpinning principles often are shared.

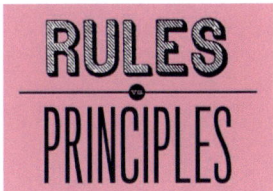

Product management

The trend among IT organizations to use a product management terminology and adopt ways of working from other domains like engineering or manufacturing is clear. A quote from the ITIL 4 Foundation book can be used to show this: "The services that an organization provides are based on one or more of its products. Organizations own or have access to a variety of resources. Products are configurations of these resources, created by the organization, that will potentially be valuable for its customers."

This is not new as it was already partly introduced in previous versions of ITIL but makes ITIL 4 even more relevant and easier to relate to the emerging agile movement with its strong emphasis on product development.

KEY CONCEPTS OF SERVICE MANAGEMENT

Understand the key terms and concepts of service management

Introduction

Most organizations need to address service management challenges and utilize the potential of modern technology. ITIL 4 is designed to ensure a flexible, coordinated and integrated system for the effective governance and management of IT-enabled services.

Key terms defined and important concepts of service management introduced here include:
- organizations, service providers, service consumers, and other stakeholders
- products and services
- the nature of value and value co-creation
- service relationships
- value: outcomes, costs, and risks.

These concepts apply to all organizations and services, regardless of their nature and underpinning technology.

What is service management?

Definition: Service management
A set of specialized organizational capabilities for enabling value for customers in the form of services.

Developing these capabilities requires an understanding of:
- the nature of value
- the nature and scope of the stakeholders involved
- how value creation is enabled through services.

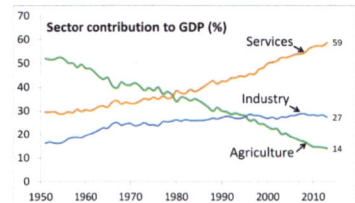

Services and products

The central component of service management is, of course, the service.

Definition: Service
A means of enabling value co-creation by facilitating outcomes that customers want to achieve, without the customer having to manage specific costs and risks.

The services that an organization provides are based on one or more of its products. Organizations own or have access to a variety of resources. Products are configurations of these resources, created by the organization, that will potentially be valuable for its customers.

Definition: Product
A configuration of an organization's resources designed to offer value for a consumer.

Services offerings

Service providers present their services to consumers in the form of service offerings, which describe one or more services based on one or more products.

Definition: Service offering

A description of one or more services, designed to address the needs of a target consumer group. A service offering may include goods, access to resources, and service actions.

Component	Description	Examples
Goods	Supplied to the consumer Ownership is transferred to the consumer Consumer takes responsibility for future use	A mobile phone A physical server
Access to resources	Ownership is not transferred to the consumer Access is granted or licensed to the consumer under agreed terms and conditions The consumer can only access the resources during the agreed consumption period and according to other agreed service terms	Access to the mobile network, or to network storage
Service actions	Performed by the service provider to address a consumer's needs Performed according to an agreement with the consumer	User support Replacement of a piece of equipment

Value creation

The **purpose of an organization** is to **create value** for stakeholders.

The term **'value'** is commonly used in service management, and it is a key focus of ITIL 4; it must therefore be clearly defined.

Definition: Value
Value is the perceived benefits, usefulness and importance of something

Value creation is a balancing act involving **outcomes**, **costs** and **risks.**

Note: Value can be subjective and therefore different according to each stakeholder!

Service providers and consumers

Service providers:
Can be **external** or **internal.** Could be selling services on the **open market** to **other businesses**, or to **individual consumers.**

Service providers can be **part of** a service alliance, collaborating to provide services to consumer organizations.

Service consumers:
When **receiving services**, an organization takes on the role of the service consumer.

It is a **generic role** that is used to simplify, in practice, more roles involved such as **customers**, **users** and **sponsors**. These roles can be **combined**.

*Clear understanding of **who its consumers are** in a given situation and who the other stakeholders are in the associated **service relationships**. These roles may have different expectations from services, and **different definitions of value**.*

Key stakeholders

Definition: Organization
A person or a group of people that has its own functions with responsibilities, authorities, and relationships to achieve its objectives.

Definition: Customer
A person who defines the requirements for a service and takes responsibility for the outcomes of service consumption.

Definition: User
A person who uses services.

Definition: Sponsor
A person who authorizes budget for service consumption.

Other stakeholders and value

A **key focus** of service management, and of ITIL, is the way that organizations **co-create value** with their consumers through **service relationships**. Beyond the consumer and provider roles, there are many **other stakeholders that are important to value creation**.

Stakeholder	Example of value for stakeholder
Service consumers	Benefits achieved; costs and risks optimized
Service provider	Funding from the consumer; business development; image improvement
Service provider employees	Financial and non-financial incentives; career and professional development; sense of purpose
Society and community	Employment; taxes; organizations' contribution to the development of the community
Charity organizations	Financial and non-financial contributions from other organizations
Shareholders	Financial benefits, such as dividends; sense of assurance and stability

It is important that relationships with all key stakeholders are understood and managed.

Service relationships

Service relationships are established between two or more organizations to create value.

The roles of service provider and service consumer are not mutually exclusive, and organizations typically both provide and consume a number of services at any given time.

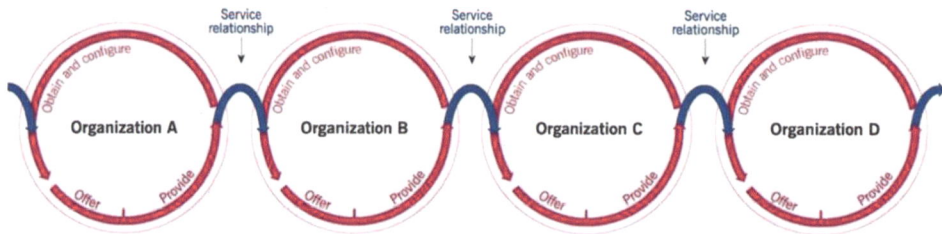

Service relationships

Definition: Service relationship management consists of **joint activities** performed by a service provider and a service consumer **to ensure continual value co-creation** based on agreed and available service offerings.

Definition: Service provisioning consists of activities performed by a service provider to provide services. This includes provision of access to resources, fulfillment of service actions, resource management and service performance and continual improvement

Definition: Service consumption consists of activities performed by a service consumer to consume services. This includes the management of the consumers resources, utilization of providers resources, requesting of service actions and acquiring of goods

Differentiate output and outcome

It is important to differentiate between output and outcome of services.

Definition: Output
A tangible or intangible deliverable of an activity.

Definition: Outcome
A result for a stakeholder enabled by one or more outputs.

Service providers should **help their consumers to achieve outcomes**.
It **can be difficult** for the provider **to fully understand the outcomes** that the consumer wants to achieve.

*Some service providers **predict** or even **create demand** for certain outcomes, forming a target group for their services.*

Two types of costs to understand

Definition: Cost
The amount of money spent on a specific activity or resource.

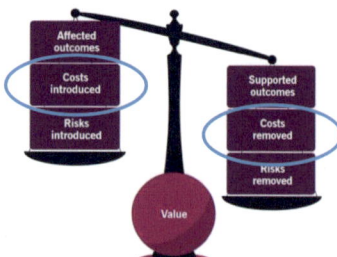

From the service consumers perspective there are two types:
Costs removed from the consumer by the service (a part of the value proposition).

Costs introduced or imposed on the consumer by the service (the costs of service consumption). Some consumers describe this as what they have to 'invest' to consume the service.

Key concepts of service management © AXELOS Limited and Van Haren Publishing

Two types of risk to understand

Definition: Risk
A possible **event** that could cause **harm** or **loss** or make it more difficult to achieve objectives. Can also be defined as "**uncertainty of outcome**".

From the service consumers perspective there are two types:
Risks removed from the consumer by the service (a part of the value proposition).

Risks introduced or imposed on the consumer by the service (risks of service consumption).

Balanced approach needed to risk reduction throughout the service relationship.

Key concepts of service management © AXELOS Limited and Van Haren Publishing

Definitions of utility and warranty

Utility:
The **functionality** offered by a product or service to **meet a particular need**.

Utility can be summarized as **'what the service does'** and can be used to determine whether a service is **'fit for purpose'**.

To have utility, a service must either support the **performance** of the consumer or **remove constraints** from the consumer. Many services do both.

Warranty:
Assurance that a product or service will meet **agreed requirements**.

How the service performs and can be used to determine whether a service is **'fit for use'**.

Often a formal **agreement**, related to **service levels**, or a **marketing message** or **brand image**. A 'warranty', if **all** defined and **agreed** conditions are met in areas such as **availability, capacity, security** and **continuity** levels of service.

Both *are essential for a service to facilitate its desired outcomes and create value.*

Summary

We have just talked about:

- ✓ This section has covered the key concepts in service management, in particular the nature of value and value co-creation, organizations, products and services

- ✓ It has explored the often complex relationships between service providers and consumers, and the various stakeholders involved.

- ✓ The chapter has also covered the key components of consumer value: outcomes, costs and risks, and how important it is to understand the needs of the customer when designing and delivering services

- ✓ These concepts will be built upon throughout this training, and guidance provided on applying them in practical and flexible ways

- ✓ After completing this section you should be able to recall several definitions, understand and be able to describe several key concepts.

Identify the missing word(s) in the following sentence

A service is a means of enabling value co-creation by facilitating [?] that customers want to achieve.

- A. the warranty
- B. outcomes
- C. the utility
- D. outputs

Which is the definition of warranty?

- A. A tangible or intangible deliverable that is produced by carrying out an activity
- B. The assurance that a product or service will meet agreed requirements
- C. A possible event that could cause harm or loss, or make it more difficult to achieve objectives
- D. The functionality offered by a product or service to meet a particular need

A service provider describes a package that includes a laptop with software, licenses, and support.

What is this package an example of?

- A. Value
- B. An outcome
- C. Warranty of a service
- D. A service offering

What are the two types of cost that a service consumer should evaluate?

- A. The cost of creating the service, and the cost charged for the service
- B. The costs removed by the service, and the costs imposed by the service
- C. The cost of provisioning the service, and the cost of improving the service
- D. The cost of purchasing software, and the cost of purchasing hardware

Course schedule
- Day 1: Key concepts of service management
  - Value creation, outcomes, costs and risks
  - Services and service relationships
  - The four dimensions
  - The ITIL service value system
  - The activities of the service value chain
  - The nature and use of the guiding principles
- Day 2: Selected ITIL practices and key terms
  - Service management practices
  - General practices
  - Technical practices

FOUR DIMENSIONS

Understand the four dimensions of service management

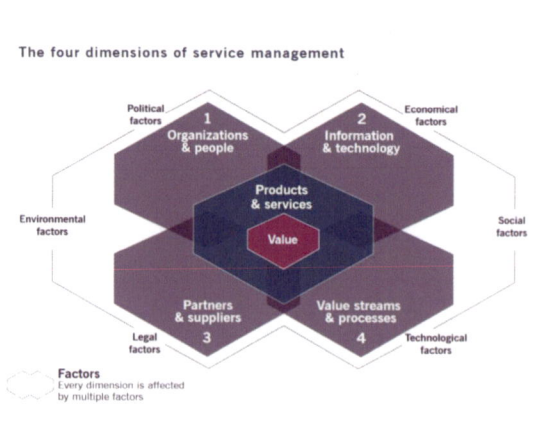

The four dimensions of service management

Four dimensions

Previously referred to as "the 4 P's of ITSM" these dimensions are well used in ITIL. They are still relevant to, and impact upon, **all practices**, the entire **service value chain** and the whole **Service Value System (SVS)**.

These **four dimensions** are:
- ✓ **Organizations and people**
- ✓ **Information and technology**
- ✓ **Partners and suppliers**
- ✓ **Value streams and processes**

*Note: The four dimensions do **not** have **sharp boundaries** and **may overlap**, and apply to **all services** being managed!*

Organizations should **holistically** consider **all aspects** of their behavior, but will often become **too focused on one** dimension in their initiatives and neglect others.

---

1. Organizations and people

The first dimension of service management – **organizations & people** – is important to ensure that the way an organization is **structured** and **managed**, as well as **its roles, responsibilities, systems of authority** and **communication** are well-defined and **support** its over-all **strategy** and **operating** model.

Other important aspects of this dimension are:
- ✓ A **culture** that supports its **objectives**, **capacity** and **competence** among its workforce
- ✓ Leaders advocate **values** that **motivate people** – the **key element**
- ✓ Understanding the **interfaces**, to ensure proper levels of **collaboration** and **coordination**
- ✓ **Everyone** should have a focus on **value creation** and **broad general knowledge**

Adopting the ITIL guiding principles can be a good starting point

2. Information and technology

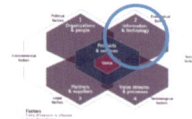

The technologies that support service management include, but are not limited to, workflow management systems, knowledge bases, inventory systems, communication systems and analytical tools.

In the context of a **specific IT service**, this dimension includes the information created, managed and used in the course of service provision and consumption, and the technologies that support and enable that service.

The IT architecture, including applications, databases, communication systems and their integrations and the use of technology is a business differentiator.

The culture of an organization may have significant impact on the technologies it chooses

Information management

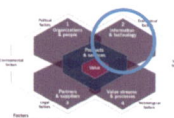

Information management is a means of enabling business value and **information** is generally the **key output** of a majority of IT services provided.

Another **key consideration** in this dimension is **how information is exchanged** between different services and service components

The information architecture needs to be **well-understood** and **continually optimized** – taking into account such criteria as; **availability**, **reliability**, **accessibility**, **timeliness**, **accuracy**, and **relevance** of the information provided.

Focus for this dimension are also **security**, **regulatory** and **compliance requirements**.

Technology - good questions to ask

- Is this technology compatible with the current architecture of the organization and its customer(s)?
- Do the different technology products used work together?
- How are emerging technologies (such as machine learning, artificial intelligence and Internet of Things) likely to disrupt the service or the organization?
- Does this technology raise any regulatory or other compliance issues with the organization's policies and information security controls, or those of its customers?
- Is this a technology that will continue to be viable in the foreseeable future?
- Is the organization willing to accept the risk of using aging technology, or of embracing emerging or unproven technology?
- Does this technology align with the strategy of the provider, or its service consumers?
- Does the organization have the right skills across its staff and suppliers to support and maintain the technology?
- Does this technology have sufficient automation capabilities to ensure it can be efficiently developed, deployed and operated?
- Does this technology offer additional capabilities that might be leveraged for other products or services?
- Does this technology introduce new risks or constraints to the organization (for example, locking it into a specific vendor)?

ITSM - cloud computing

Definition: Cloud computing
A model for enabling on-demand network access to a shared pool of configurable computing resources that can be rapidly provided with minimal management effort or provider interaction.

Cloud computing **changes** service architecture and distribution of **responsibilities** between service consumers, service providers and their partners. It may enable significantly **faster deployment** of new and changed services, thus supporting **high velocity** service delivery.

Considering the influence of cloud computing on organizations, it is important to make decisions about the use of this model at the strategic level of the organization, **involving all levels of stakeholders**, from governance to operations.

Cloud computing impact on ITSM

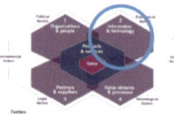

Replaces some infrastructure, previously managed by the service provider, with a partner's cloud service.

Decreases or removes the need for infrastructure management expertise and resources.

Shifts focus of service monitoring and control from in-house infrastructure to the cloud.

Changes cost structures of the service provider, removing specific capital expenditures and introducing new operating expenditures.

Introduces higher requirements for network availability and security.

Introduces new security and compliance risks and requirements, applicable to both the service provider and their partner providing the cloud service.

Provides users with opportunities to scale service consumption using self-service, via simple standard requests, or even without any requests.

Cloud computing affects practices

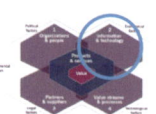

Practices that are affected by cloud computing, include, but are not limited to:
- ✓ service level management
- ✓ measurement and reporting
- ✓ information security management
- ✓ service continuity management
- ✓ supplier management
- ✓ incident management
- ✓ problem management
- ✓ service request management
- ✓ service configuration management

3. Partners and supplier

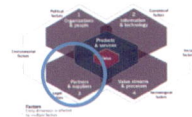

Every organization and every service **depends**, to some extent, on **services provided by other organizations**.

This dimension covers relationships with other organizations that are **involved** in the **design**, **development**, **deployment**, **delivery**, **support** and/or **continual improvement** of services.

Contracts and agreements - This ranges from formal contracts with clear separation of responsibilities, to flexible partnerships where parties share common goals and risks, and collaborate to achieve desired outcomes.

Form of cooperation	Outputs	Responsibility for the outputs	Responsibility for achievement of the outcomes	Level of formality	Examples
Goods supply	Goods supplied	Supplier	Customer	Formal supply contract/invoices	Procurement of computers and phones
Service delivery	Services delivered	Provider	Customer	Formal agreements and flexible cases	Cloud computing (infrastructure of platform as a service)
Service partnership	Value co-created	Shared between provider and customer	Shared between provider and customer	Shared goals, generic agreements, flexible case-based arrangements	Employee onboarding (shared between HR, facilities and IT)

Different strategies for cooperation

Forms of **cooperation** depends on strategy and objectives for customer relationships. **Strategy** to using partners and suppliers should be based on its **goals**, **culture** and **business environment**. Influencing factors include:

Strategic focus - to focus on core competencies or to stay as self-sufficient as possible
Corporate culture - long-standing cultural bias is difficult to change
Resource scarcity - resources or skillsets in short supply are acquired from suppliers
Cost concerns - more economical to source a particular requirement from a supplier
Subject matter expertise - less risky to use a supplier that already has an expertise
External constrains - regulation or policy constraints might impact a strategy
Demand patterns - customer activity or demand for services might be seasonal or variable

Service Integration and Management

One method an organization may use the partners and suppliers dimension is **service integration and management (SIAM)**. This uses an integrator to help **ensure** that **service relationships** are **properly coordinated**.

Service integration and management **may be kept inside** the organization, but can also be **delegated** to a **trusted partner**.

'as a service' – a bundle of goods and services to a single product that can be consumed as a utility

4. Value streams and processes

The value streams and processes dimension applies **to both** the **Service Value System (SVS)** in general, and to specific **products** and **services**. In **both contexts** it defines activities, workflows, controls and procedures needed to achieve agreed objectives. The dimension **focuses on** what **activities** the organization undertakes, and how they are **organized**, as well as how the organization ensures that it is **enabling value creation** for all stakeholders **efficiently** and **effectively**.

ITIL gives service providers an **operating model** that **covers all** the **key activities** required to effectively manage products and services, called the **ITIL service value chain**.

The service value chain operating model is **generic**; however, in practice it can **follow different patterns**. These **patterns** within the value chain operation are **called value streams**.

Value streams

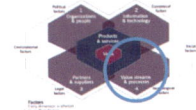

Definition: Value stream
A **series of steps** an organization undertakes to
create and deliver products and services to consumers.

A value stream is a **combination of** the organization's **value chain activities**. Identifying and understanding the organizations value streams is critical to improving its performance. Structuring its service and product portfolios around value streams gives organizations a **clear picture** of what they deliver and how, and how to continually improve.

Value stream optimization may include **process automation** or adoption of emerging technologies and ways of working to gain efficiencies or enhance user experience and eliminate waste. Value streams should be **adoptable** and **continually improved**.

Processes

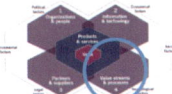

Definition: Process
A set of interrelated or interacting **activities** that transform inputs into outputs. A process takes one or more **defined inputs** and turns them **into defined outputs**. Processes define the **sequence** of actions and their dependencies.

Processes **describe** what is **done to accomplish an objective**, and well-defined processes can improve productivity within and across organizations. They are usually **detailed** in **procedures**, which outline who is involved in the process, and **work instructions**, which explain how they are carried out.

The same structure (of the value chain, value streams, processes, procedures and work instructions) applies to services: to successfully **create, deliver** and **improve a service.**

External factors

Other factors that influence the four dimensions are:
- ✓ Political factors
- ✓ Economical factors
- ✓ Social factors
- ✓ Technological factors
- ✓ Legal factors
- ✓ Environmental factors

Collectively, these factors influence how organizations configure their resources and address the four dimensions of service management.

Political	Economic	Social
• Tax policies • Fiscal policy • Trade tariffs • Change of government • Local government policy (eg planning consents)	• Inflation rate • Interest rates • Foreign exchange rates, • Economic growth patterns	• Cultural trends • Demographics • Employee expectations • Population analytics • Buying trends • Seasonal behaviors
Technological	**Legal**	**Environmental**
• Automation • Research and development • Technical awareness in the market • Impact of new media	• Consumer laws • Health and safety standards, • Labour laws etc. • Trade barriers	• Geographical location • Climate change • Environmental offsets • Emissions legislation • Green agenda

Four Dimensions of service management — © AXELOS Limited and Van Haren Publishing — 45

Summary

We have just talked about:

- ✓ This section has covered the four dimensions of ITSM:
  1. Organizations and people
  2. Technology and information
  3. Partners and suppliers
  4. Value streams and processes
- ✓ Other external factors to consider include:
  - Political factors
  - Economical factors
  - Social factors
  - Technological factors
  - Legal factors
  - Environmental factors
- ✓ Every dimension is affected by multiple factors and influence how service providers operate

Four Dimensions of service management — © AXELOS Limited and Van Haren Publishing — 46

Which service management dimension is focused on activities and how these are coordinated?

A. Organizations and people

B. Information and technology

C. Partners and suppliers

D. Value streams and processes

Which is NOT a key focus of the 'information and technology' dimension?

A. Security and compliance

B. Communication systems and knowledge bases

C. Workflow management and inventory systems

D. Roles and responsibilities

Course schedule

- Day 1: Key concepts of service management
  - ✓ Value creation, outcomes, costs and risks
  - ✓ Services and service relationships
  - ✓ The four dimensions
  - The ITIL service value system
  - The activities of the service value chain
  - The nature and use of the guiding principles
- Day 2: Selected ITIL practices and key terms
  - Service management practices
  - General practices
  - Technical practices

ITIL SERVICE VALUE SYSTEM

Understand the purpose and components of the ITIL service value system (SVS)

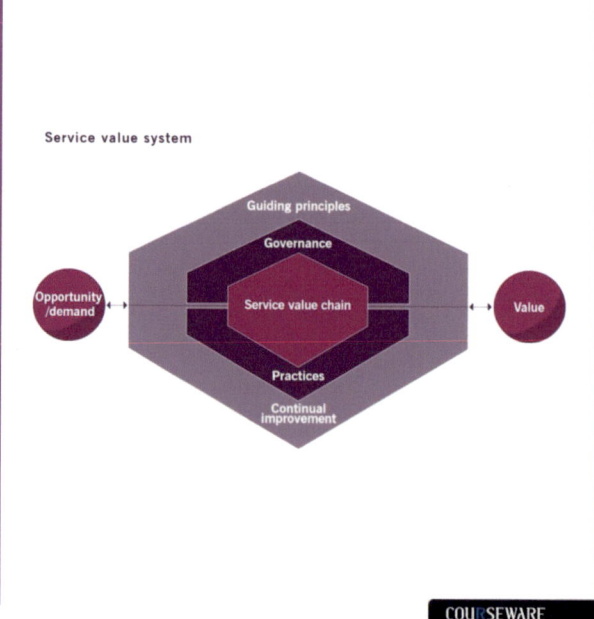

ITIL service value system (SVS)

To enable value creation, **all** the **components and activities** of the organization need to **work together as a system**. The three main parts of the ITIL SVS are:

- ✓ **Inputs** to the system:
  - **Opportunity** and **demand**
- ✓ **Components** of the system:
  - **Guiding principles**
  - **Governance**
  - **Service value chain**
  - **Practices**
  - **Continual improvement**
- ✓ **Outputs** of the system:
  - Achievement of **objectives** and **value**

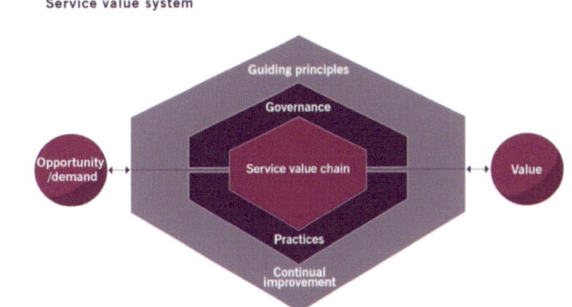

Service value system

Purpose of the SVS

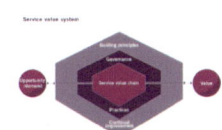

Purpose:
- ✓ To ensure that the organization continually co-creates value with all stakeholders through the use and management of products and services.

The ITIL SVS describes how all the components and activities of the organization work together as a system to enable value creation. These activities represent the steps an organization takes in the creation of value. Each activity contributes to the value chain by transforming specific inputs into outputs.

To convert inputs into outputs, the value chain activities use different combinations of ITIL practices (sets of resources designed for performing certain types of work). Each activity may draw upon internal or third-party resources, processes, skills, and competencies from one or more practices.

Inputs and outputs of the SVS

Each organization's SVS has interfaces with other organizations, forming an **ecosystem**. The inputs and outputs of the SVS can be described further as:

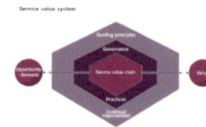

Inputs:
- ✓ **Opportunity** – represents options or possibilities to add value for stakeholders or otherwise improve the organization
- ✓ **Demand** – need or desire for products and services among internal and external consumers

Outcome:
- ✓ **Value** – the perceived benefits, usefulness and importance of something

ITIL SVS can enable creation of different types of value for a wide group of stakeholders.

Components of the SVS

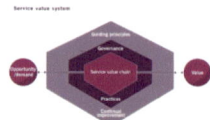

Guiding principles
- ✓ Recommendations that can guide an organization in all circumstances, regardless of changes in its goals, strategies, type of work, or management structure.

Governance
- ✓ The means by which an organization is directed and controlled.

Service value chain
- ✓ A set of interconnected activities that an organization performs to deliver a valuable product or service to its consumers and to facilitate value realization.

Practices
- ✓ Sets of organizational resources designed for performing work or accomplishing an objective.

Continual improvement
- ✓ A recurring organizational activity performed at all levels to ensure that an organization's performance continually meets stakeholders' expectations.

Challenges

Components and activities, together with the organization's resources, can be **configured** and **reconfigured** in **multiple combinations** in a **flexible** way as circumstances change. But this requires the **integration** and **coordination** of activities, practices, teams, authorities and responsibilities and all parties to be truly effective.

Challenges:
- ✓ **Organizational silos** makes it hard to work effectively and efficiently with a shared vision, or to become more agile and resilient
- ✓ **Silos can be resistant to change** and **prevent easy access to the information** and **specialized expertise**, which can reduce efficiency and increase cost and risk
- ✓ Silos also make **communication** or **collaboration** more difficult across groups.

Challenges addressed with SVS

The ITIL SVS has been specifically **architected** to **enable flexibility** and **discourage** siloed working. It does not form a **fixed**, rigid **structure**. There are examples of value streams, but they are **not definite or prescriptive**.

Organizations should be able to define and redefine their value streams in a **flexible, yet safe** and **efficient** manner. This requires **continual improvement** activity to be carried out at all levels of the organization.

The **guiding principles create a foundation** for a shared culture across the organization. ITIL SVS **supports many work approaches**, such as Agile, DevOps and Lean, as well as traditional process and project management, with a **flexible value-oriented operating model**.

Organizational agility and resilience

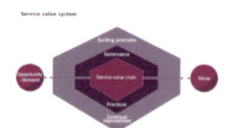

Organizational agility is the ability of an organization to **move** and **adapt quickly, flexibly** and **decisively** to support **internal changes.**

Organizational resilience is the ability of an organization to **anticipate, prepare for, respond to** and **adapt to** both **incremental changes** and sudden **disruptions** from an external perspective. It **requires** a common **understanding** of **priorities** and **objectives.**

Successful organizations must achieve **agility** and **resilience** to **support internal changes**, and **withstand** or even **thrive** in **changing external circumstances**. They must also be **part of larger ecosystems, delivering, coordinating** and **consuming** products and services.

The SVS **provides** the **means to achieve organizational agility** and **resilience** and to facilitate the adoption of a strong unified direction, focused on value and understood by all.

Summary

We have just talked about:

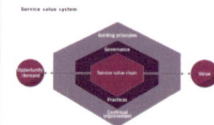

- ✓ This section has covered the ITIL Service Value System (SVS) and its purpose, function, structure and business value
- ✓ The three main parts of the SVS and their content:
  Inputs:
  - *Opportunity* and *demand*
  Components:
  - *Guiding principles*
  - *Governance*
  - *Service value chain*
  - *Practices*
  - *Continual improvement*
  Outcome:
  - *Value to stakeholders*
- ✓ The reason for the architecture of the SVS and how it addresses challenges with a siloed approach

Which ITIL concept describes governance?

A. The seven guiding principles

B. The four dimensions of service management

C. The service value chain

D. The service value system

Course schedule
- Day 1: Key concepts of service management
  - ✓ Value creation, outcomes, costs and risks
  - ✓ Services and service relationships
  - ✓ The four dimensions
  - ✓ The ITIL service value system
  - • The activities of the service value chain
  - • The nature and use of the guiding principles
- Day 2: Selected ITIL practices and key terms
  - • Service management practices
  - • General practices
  - • Technical practices

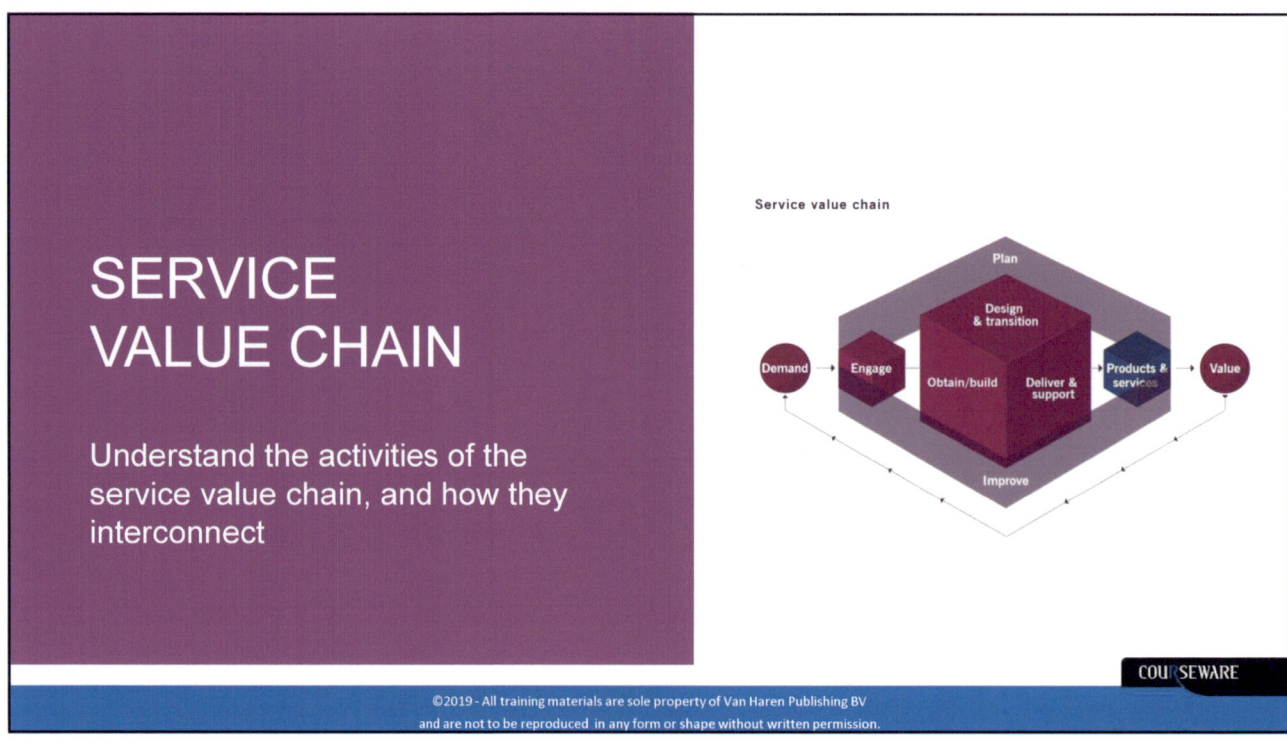

A central element of the SVS

The **service value chain**, an operating model which **outlines** the **key activities** required to **respond** to **demand** and **facilitate value realization** through the **creation** and **management** of **products** and **services**. Its **six key activities** are:
- ✓ **Plan**
- ✓ **Improve**
- ✓ **Engage**
- ✓ **Design & transition**
- ✓ **Obtain/build**
- ✓ **Deliver & support.**

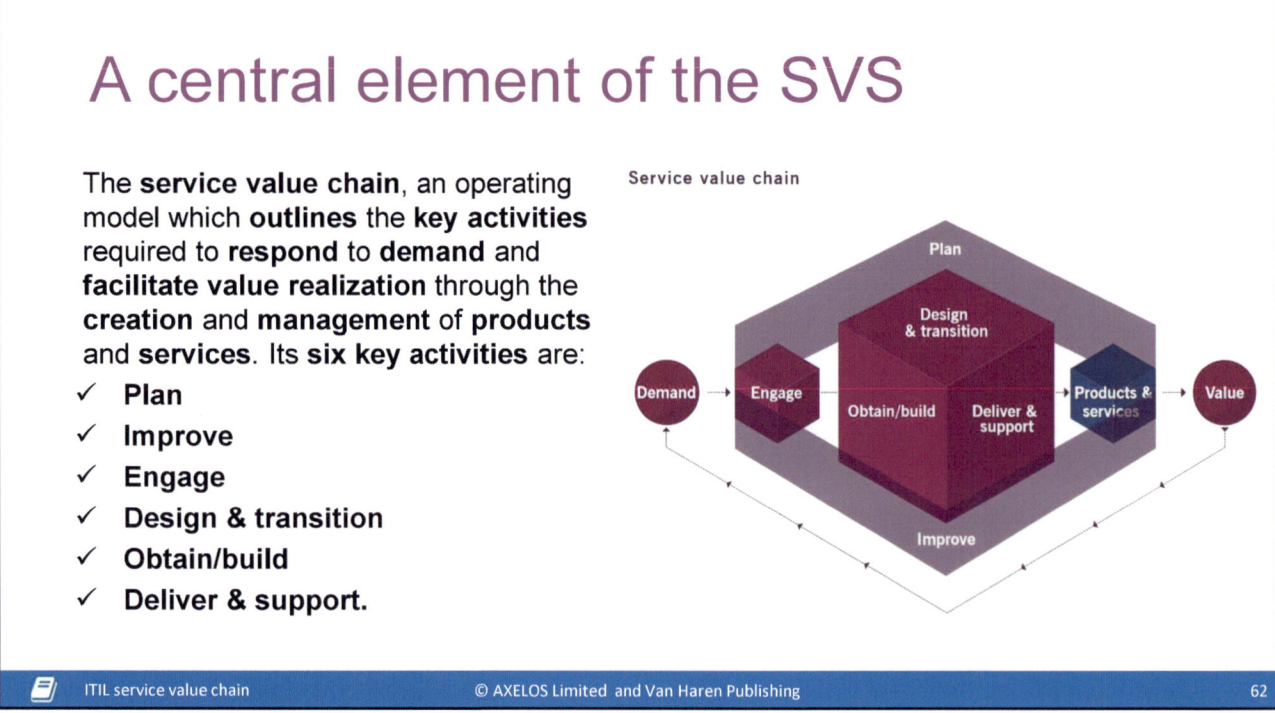

The service value chain

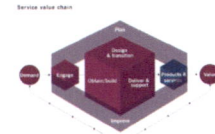

The **activities** are **connected to**, and **interact with** one another, with each activity **receiving** and **providing triggers** for further **actions** to be taken.

To convert **inputs** into **outputs**, the value chain activities use different combinations of **ITIL practices** (sets of resources designed for performing certain types of work).

For example:
The **engage** *value chain* **activity** *might* **draw upon** *a number of* **practices** *including* **supplier management, service desk management, relationship management** *and* **service request management** *to respond to* new **demands** *for products and services, decisions, or information* **from various stakeholders***.*

Service value streams

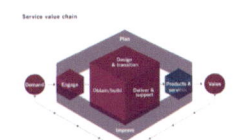

Service value streams are specific **combinations** of **activities** and **practices**, and each one is **designed for a particular scenario**. Once designed, value streams should be subject to **continual improvement**.

Example of generic **practices** that can be used to support many different scenarios:
- ✓ Business analysis
- ✓ Development
- ✓ Testing
- ✓ Release and deployment
- ✓ Support.

Note: Although the high-level steps are universal, different products and clients need different streams of work.

These practices are **applied differently**, depending on scenario and product or service, in **different value streams** and **combine different practices** and **value chain activities**.

Plan

The purpose of this value chain activity is to ensure a **shared understanding** of the **vision**, current **status** and improvement **direction** for all four dimensions and all products and services across the organization.

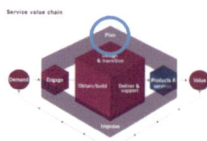

The **key inputs** to this activity are:
- ✓ **policies**, **requirements**, and **constraints** provided by the organization's **governing body**
- ✓ **consolidated demands** and **opportunities** provided by *engage*
- ✓ value chain **performance information**, **improvement initiatives**, and **plans** provided by *improve*
- ✓ **improvement status** reports from *improve*
- ✓ **knowledge and information** about **new and changed products** and **services** from *design and transition*, and *obtain/build*
- ✓ **knowledge and information** about **third-party** service components from *engage*.

Improve

The purpose of this value chain activity is to **ensure continual improvement** of products, services and practices **across all value chain activities** and the **four dimensions of service management**.

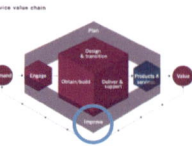

The **key inputs** to this activity are:
- ✓ **product and service performance information** provided by *deliver and support*
- ✓ **stakeholders' feedback** provided by *engage*
- ✓ **performance information** and improvement opportunities provided by *all value chain activities*
- ✓ **knowledge and information** about **new and changed products** and services from *design and transition* and *obtain/build*
- ✓ **knowledge and information** about **third party service components** from *engage*.

Engage

The purpose is to provide a good understanding of stakeholder needs, transparency, and continual engagement and **good relationships with all stakeholders**.

The **key inputs** to this activity are:
- ✓ **Product** and **service portfolio** provided by *plan*
- ✓ **High level demand** and **detailed requirements** for **services** and **products** provided by **customers**
- ✓ **Incidents, service requests, feedback** and **market opportunities** from **customers** and **users**
- ✓ **Cooperation opportunities** and **feedback** provided by **partners** and **suppliers**
- ✓ **Contract** and **agreement requirements** from *all value chain activities*
- ✓ **Knowledge** and **information** about **third party service components** from **suppliers** and **partners**
- ✓ **Product** and **service performance information** and of **user support tasks** from *deliver and support*
- ✓ **Improvements initiatives** and **plans** and their **status** reports from *improve*.

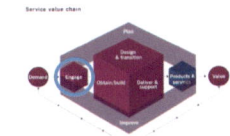

Design and transition

The purpose is to ensure that products and services **continually meet stakeholder expectations** for **quality**, **costs**, and **time to market**.

The **key inputs** to this activity are:
- ✓ **portfolio decisions** provided by *plan*
- ✓ **architectures** and **policies** provided by *plan*
- ✓ **product** and **service requirements** provided by *engage*
- ✓ **improvement initiatives** and **plans** provided by *improve*
- ✓ **improvement status** reports from *improve*
- ✓ **service performance information** provided by *deliver and support*, and *improve*
- ✓ **service components** from *obtain/build*
- ✓ **knowledge** and **information** about **third-party service components** from *engage*
- ✓ **knowledge** and **information** about **new** and **changed products** and **services** from *obtain/build*.

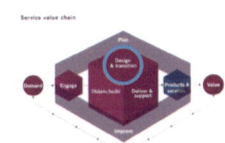

Obtain/build

The purpose is to ensure that service components are **available when** and **where** they are **needed**, and **meet agreed specifications**.

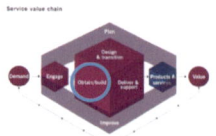

The **key inputs** to this activity are:
- ✓ **architectures** and **policies** provided by *plan*
- ✓ **contracts** and **agreements** with **external** and **internal suppliers** and **partners** provided by *engage*
- ✓ **goods** and **services** provided by **external** and **internal suppliers** and **partners**
- ✓ **requirements** and **specifications** provided by *design and transition*
- ✓ **improvement initiatives**, **plans** and **improvement status** reports provided by *improve*
- ✓ **change** or **project initiation requests** provided by *engage*
- ✓ **change requests** provided by *deliver and support*
- ✓ **knowledge** and **information** about **new** or **changed products** and **services** from *design & transition*
- ✓ **knowledge** and **information** about **third-party service components** from *engage*.

 ITIL service value chain © AXELOS Limited and Van Haren Publishing

Deliver and support

The purpose is to ensure that services are **delivered** and **supported** according to **agreed specifications** and **stakeholders' expectations**.

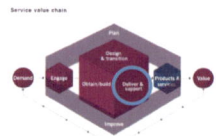

The **key inputs** to this activity are:
- ✓ **new** and **changed products** and **services** provided by *design and transition*
- ✓ **contracts** and **agreements** with **external** and **internal suppliers** and **partners** provided by *engage*
- ✓ **service components** provided by *obtain/build*
- ✓ **improvement initiatives** and **plans** provided by *improve*
- ✓ **improvement status** reports from *improve*
- ✓ **user support tasks** provided by *engage*
- ✓ **knowledge** and **information** about **new** and **changed service components** and **services** from *design and transition*, and *obtain/build*
- ✓ **knowledge** and **information** about **third-party service components** from *engage*.

 ITIL service value chain © AXELOS Limited and Van Haren Publishing

Agile ITSM

For an organization to be successful, it must be able to **adapt** to **changing circumstances** while **remaining functional** and **effective**. Many principles of Agile development can and should be applied to service management.

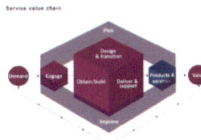

Agile software development usually includes:
- ✓ **Continually evolving** requirements, collected through feedback analysis and direct observation
- ✓ Breaking development work into **small increments and iterations**
- ✓ Establishing *product-based cross-functional teams*
- ✓ **Visually presented** (Kanban) and **regularly discussed** (daily stand-ups) work progress
- ✓ Presenting a working (or the minimum **viable) software** to the stakeholders at **end of each iteration**.

If applied successfully, **agile** software development **enables fast responses** to the **evolving needs** of **service consumers**.

Agile ITSM

However, in many organizations, agile software development has not provided the expected benefits, often due to **lack of agility in the other phases of the service lifecycle**.

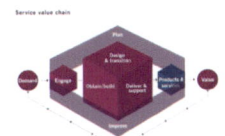

Overall performance of the value chain is **defined by** that of the **slowest part**.

A holistic approach to the service value chain should be adopted to make sure that the service provider is **agile throughout the service lifecycle**.

If adopted as a key principle, agility can **enable** an organization to survive and prosper in a constantly changing environment. **Applied** in a **fragmented** way, agile methods can become a **costly** and wasteful complication.

Summary

We have just talked about:

- ✓ This section has covered the service value chain, an operating model which outlines the key activities required to respond to demand and facilitate value realization through the creation and management of products and services.
- ✓ The six key activities are:
  - Plan
  - Improve
  - Engage
  - Design and transition
  - Obtain/build
  - Deliver and support
- ✓ The service value streams that are specific combinations of activities and practices, and each one is designed for a particular scenario. Once designed, value streams should be subject to continual improvement.
- ✓ The need for, and positive influence possible, by integrating agile ways of working with ITSM.

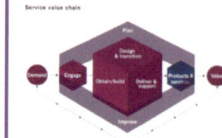

ITIL service value chain

Which value chain activity creates service components?

A. Improve

B. Engage

C. Obtain/build

D. Deliver and support

Which statement about the value chain activities is CORRECT?

A. Every practice belongs to a specific value chain activity

B. A specific combination of value chain activities and practices forms a service relationship

C. Service value chain activities form a single flow that enables value creation

D. Each value chain activity contributes to the value chain by transforming specific inputs into outputs

---

Which value chain activity includes negotiation of contracts and agreements with suppliers and partners?

A. Engage

B. Design and transition

C. Obtain/build

D. Deliver and support

Course schedule
- Day 1: Key concepts of service management
  - Value creation, outcomes, costs and risks
  - Services and service relationships
  - The four dimensions
  - The ITIL service value system
  - The activities of the service value chain
  - The nature and use of the guiding principles
- Day 2: Selected ITIL practices and key terms
  - Service management practices
  - General practices
  - Technical practices

ITIL GUIDING PRINCIPLES

Understand how the ITIL guiding principles can help an organization adopt and adapt service management

What is an ITIL guiding principle?

It is a recommendation **that guides** an organization **in all circumstances**, regardless of changes in its goals, strategies, type of work, or management structure. A guiding principle is **universal** and **enduring**. But **not prescriptive or mandatory.**

It **embodies the core messages** of ITIL and of service management in general, **supporting** successful **actions** and good **decisions** of **all types** and at **all levels**.

It helps organizations to **adopt** a service management approach and **adapt** ITIL guidance to their **own specific needs** and **circumstances** and encourage and support organizations in **continual improvement at all levels.**

Many of these principles **are reflected** in many **other** frameworks, methods, standards, philosophies and/or bodies of knowledge.

Principle interaction and relevance

ITIL guiding principles, **interact with** and **depend upon each other**.

Organizations therefore should not use just one or two of the principles consider the relevance of each of them and how they apply together.

Not all principles will be critical in every situation, but they should all be each occasion to determine how appropriate they are.

Similarly, making use of appropriate **feedback** is key to **collaboration**, what will **truly be valuable to the customer** makes it easier to keep th practical.

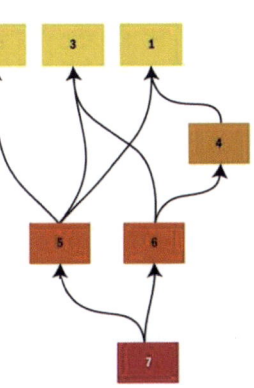

The ITIL guiding principles

Guiding principle	Description
Focus on value	Everything that the organization does needs to map, directly or indirectly, to value for the stakeholders.
Start where you are	Do not start from scratch and build something new without considering what is already available to be leveraged. The current state should be investigated and observed directly to make sure it is fully understood.
Progress iteratively with feedback	Do not attempt to do everything at once. Even huge initiatives must be accomplished iteratively.
Collaborate and promote visibility	Working together across boundaries produces results that have greater buy in, more relevance to objectives and better likelihood of long-term success. Achieving objectives requires information, understanding and trust.
Think and work holistically	Results are delivered to internal and external customers through the effective and efficient management and dynamic integration of information, technology, organization, people, practices, partners and agreements, which should all be coordinated to provide a defined value.
Keep it simple and practical	If a process, service, action or metric provides no value, or produces no useful outcome, eliminate it. Always use outcome-based thinking to produce practical solutions that deliver results.
Optimize and automate	Eliminate anything that is truly wasteful and use technology to achieve whatever it is capable of. Human intervention should only happen where it really contributes value.

The Agile methodology

A methodology that focuses on **delivery** and **evolution** of requirements from **small teams**. It is a **timeboxed**, flexible and adaptive approach focusing on **rapid** response to change.

Teams are often **self organized** and there is a high degree of **collaboration** between customers, users and development teams at every opportunity.

Possible challenges with Agile are:
- ✓ Basic **organizational** capabilities need to be established.
- ✓ **Focus on features and fixes**, rather than improving the service.
- ✓ Higher **costs over time**, less accurate time estimations and a lower quality of service delivery.
- ✓ It can result in **over-engineered** projects that have been built iteratively with no consideration for the overall service.

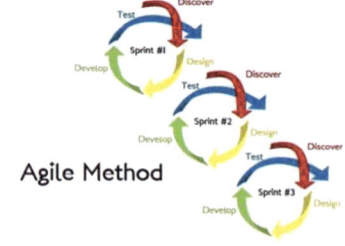

Agile Method

ITIL and Agile in cooperation

ITIL can complement Agile teams to enable more effective, faster and stable deployment within the **context of the wider service concept** and reduce ongoing cost of the service.

Together they they can lead to better **co-ordination** between agile projects and other **areas** of the service/business that might **not work with Agile methods**.

Agile shares many common themes with ITIL, and together they can support each other to produce highly **effective practices** including, but not limited to:
- ✓ **Continual improvement**
- ✓ **Problem management**
- ✓ **Change enablement**
- ✓ **Release management**
- ✓ **Deployment management.**

ITIL and DevOps in cooperation

DevOps arose from the increasing success of Agile software projects that led organizations to **release more frequently**

DevOps centers on the process of delivering software to live environments, with a focus on **unifying technical operations and delivery**.

Anyone with the responsibility for **change enablement**, **release management** and **service operations** should be a **part of the Agile team** to ensure that the team work effectively together.

All coming together

Agile methods focus on working in timeboxed iterations, which can carry a risk of introducing instability in ongoing services. As Agile focuses on automation and speed of delivery it may be beneficial for teams to also use DevOps to help ITIL and Agile practices work well together.

The Agile roles within teams can be multi-purpose and aligned to ITSM roles, for example:
- ✓ Product managers/owners can perform the role of the service owner
- ✓ Scrum masters can perform the role of the change manager
- ✓ Scrum masters are already running retrospectives and ensuring lessons are learned, which can form a part of the wider continual improvement practice.

ITIL and Agile can be great allies. An Agile team focusing on customer needs and satisfaction through the lens of the overall service will deliver greater value in a shorter amount of time.

Sets of principles compared

Agile Manifesto	ITIL guiding principles
Individuals and interactions over processes and tools	• Keep it simple and practical • Start where you are
Working software over comprehensive documentation	• Focus on value • Think and work holistically
Customer collaboration over contract negotiation	• Focus on value • Collaborate and promote visibility
Responding to change over following a plan	• Progress iteratively with feedback • Keep it simple and practical

Focus on value

Everything the organization does, should link back, directly or indirectly, to **value** for itself, its customers and other stakeholders. **Value may come in various forms**, such as revenue, customer loyalty, lower cost or growth opportunities.

Who is the service consumer?
When focusing on value, the **first step** is to know **who is being served**. In each situation the service provider must, therefore, determine **who the service consumer** is and **who the key stakeholders** are, in doing this the service provider should consider **who will receive value** from what is being delivered or improved.

> Note: Remember to address various stakeholder groups, **not only customers**.

Consumer perspective

When identified the consumer, the service provider needs to further know:
- ✓ **why** the consumer uses the services?
- ✓ **what** the services help them to do?
- ✓ **how** the services help them meet their goals?
- ✓ the role of **cost/financial** consequences for the service consumer?
- ✓ the role of **risks** for the service consumer?

Value can come **in many forms**, such as increased productivity, reduced negative impact, reduced costs, the ability to pursue new markets or a better competitive position. It is defined by the services consumer's **own needs,** achieved through the support of **intended outcomes** and **optimization** of the **costs** and **risks**. It also **changes over time** and **in different circumstances**.

The customer or user experience

An **important element** of value is the **experience** consumers have when they interact with the service and the service provider. This is often further expanded into customer experience (**CX**) or user experience (**UX**).

CX (or UX) can be defined as the entirety of the interactions a customer (or user) has with an organization and its products. This experience can **determine how the customer feels** about the organization and its **products** and **services**. This is **both objective and subjective**.

For example:
When a customer orders a product and receives what they ordered at the promised price and in the promised delivery time, the success of this aspect of their experience is objectively measurable. On the other hand, if they don't like the style or layout of the website they are ordering from, this is subjective. Another customer might really enjoy the design.

Applying the principle

Know how service **consumers use** each service
- ✓ *Collect feedback on value on an ongoing basis, not just at the beginning of the service relationship.*

Encourage a **focus on value among all staff**
- ✓ *Teach staff to be aware of who their customers are and to understand CX (and UX).*

Focus on value during normal **operational** activity as well as during **improvement** initiatives
- ✓ *The organization as a whole contributes to the value that the customer perceives, and so everybody within the organization must maximize the value they create.*

Include **focus on value in every step** of any improvement initiative
- ✓ *Everybody involved in improvement needs to understand what outcomes the initiative is trying to facilitate, how its value will be measured, and how they should be contributing to the co-creation of value.*

Start where you are

In the process of eliminating old, unsuccessful methods or services and creating something better, there can be great **temptation to remove** what has been done in the past and build something completely new.

This is **rarely necessary**, or a wise decision. On the contrary, it can be **extremely wasteful**, not only in terms of time, but also in terms of the loss of existing services, processes, people, and tools that could have significant value in the improvement effort.

Do not start over without first considering what is already available to be leveraged.

Assess where you are

Services and methods already in place should be measured and/or observed directly to properly understand their current state and what can be reused from them.

Ensure decisions are based on **accurate** information. Be aware that there is often **discrepancy** between reports and reality.

Getting **data from the source** helps to avoid assumptions.

To ensure this, remember:
- ✓ To observe activities directly.
- ✓ That there are no stupid questions.
- ✓ That different roles need to be part of the observations, and get first hand information.

The role of measurement

The **use of measurement** is important to the principle "start where you are". It should however be used to support the analysis of what has been observed rather than to replace it as over-reliance on data analytics can introduce biases and risks.

Organizations should consider a **variety of techniques to get knowledge** of their working environments. Some things can **only** be understood **through measuring** their effect, but **direct personal** observation should always be preferred.

It should be noted that the act of **measuring can** sometimes **affect the results**, making them inaccurate. **People are very creative** in finding ways **to meet the metrics** they are measured against. Therefore, metrics need to be meaningful and directly relate to the desired outcome.

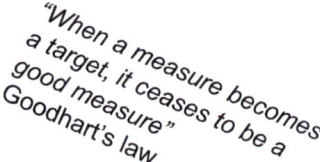
"When a measure becomes a target, it ceases to be a good measure" Goodhart's law

Applying the principle

Having a proper understanding of the current state of services and methods is important to selecting which elements to reuse, alter or build upon

Consider these advices:
- Look at **what exists** as objectively as possible, using the desired outcome **as a starting point**
- When examples of **successful** practices or services are **found**, **determine** if and **how** these can be **replicated** to achieve the **desired state**
- Apply your **risk management skills**
- Recognize that **sometimes nothing** from the current state **can be re-used**.

Progress iteratively with feedback

Resist the temptation to do everything at once. By **organizing work into smaller**, manageable sections that can be executed and completed in a timely manner, the focus on each effort will be sharper and easier to maintain **sequential or simultaneous.**

Each individual **iteration** should be both manageable and managed, ensuring that tangible results are returned in a timely manner and **built upon** to create **further improvement**.

The overall program, as well as its component iterations, must be **continually re-evaluated** and potentially revised to reflect any changes in circumstances and ensure that the focus on value has not been lost.

This re-evaluation should make use of a **wide range of feedback channels and methods** to ensure that the status of the initiative and its progress are properly understood.

The role of feedback

No improvement iteration occurs in a vacuum. Whether working to improve a service, group of services, practice, process, technical environment or other service management element. **Circumstances** can **change** and new priorities arise, and the need for the iteration may change. Seek to use **feedback before**, **throughout** and **after each iteration**.

A **feedback loop** is a situation where part of the output of an activity is used for new input. Feedback should **actively** be collected and processed **along the value chain** to understand:
- ✓ end user and customer perception of the value created.
- ✓ the efficiency and effectiveness of value chain activities.
- ✓ the effectiveness of service governance as well as management controls.
- ✓ the interfaces between the organization and its partner and supplier network.
- ✓ the demand for products and services.

Iteration and feedback together

Working in a **time-boxed**, **iterative** manner with **feedback loops** embedded into the process allows for:
- ✓ **Greater flexibility**
- ✓ **Faster** responses to customer and business needs
- ✓ The **ability to discover** and respond to failure earlier
- ✓ An overall improvement in **quality**.

*Appropriate feedback loops between the participants of an activity gives them a better understanding of where their work comes from, where their outputs go and how their actions and outputs affect the outcomes, which in turn enables them to **make better decisions.***

Applying the principle

To apply this principle successfully, consider these advices:
- ✓ **Comprehend the whole, but do something**
  Sometimes the greatest enemy to progressing iteratively is the desire to understand and account for everything. Understanding the big picture is important, but so is progress.

- ✓ **The ecosystem is constantly changing, so feedback is essential**
  Change is happening constantly, so it is important to seek and use feedback at all times and at all levels.

- ✓ **Fast does not mean incomplete**
  Just because an iteration is small enough to be done quickly does not mean that it should not include all the elements necessary for success. Create a minimal viable product, or a version which allows the maximum amount of learning with the least effort.

Collaborate and promote visibility

Involve the right people in the correct roles, efforts benefit from better buy-in, more relevance (because better information is available for decision-making) and increased likelihood of long-term success.

- ✓ **Conclusion** is generally a better policy than exclusion.
- ✓ **Silos** can occur through the behavior of individuals and teams, but also through structural causes.
- ✓ **Applying** the guiding principle of think and work holistically can help organizations to break down barriers between silos of work.
- ✓ **Recognition** of the need for genuine collaboration

Without effective collaboration, neither DevOps, Agile, Lean nor any other ITSM framework or method will work.

Transparency builds trust

Working together in a way that leads to real accomplishment requires **information**, **understanding** and **trust**.

Work and its results should be made visible, hidden agendas should be avoided and **information should be shared** to the greatest degree possible.

The more **people are aware** of what is happening and why, the more they will be willing to help. When activity's occurs behind closed doors, assumptions and rumors can prevail.

Resistance to change will often rise as staff members are unaware and therefore speculate about what is changing and how it might impact them.

Whom to collaborate with

Identifying and managing all the stakeholder groups is important, successful collaboration can be sourced within these stakeholder groups.

As the name suggests, **a stakeholder is anyone who has a stake in the activities** of the organization, including the organization itself, its customers and/or users, and many others.

The first and most obvious stakeholder group is the **customer**. Some organizations, however, do a poor job of interacting with customers.

In the end, however, the right level of collaboration with customers will lead to better outcomes for the organization, its customers and other stakeholders.

Other stakeholders to involve:

Developers working with other internal teams to ensure that what is being developed can be operated efficiently and effectively. Collaborate with technical and non-technical operational teams.

Suppliers collaborating with the organization to define its requirements and brainstorm solutions to customer problems - Internal and external suppliers collaborating with each other.

Relationship managers collaborating with service consumers to achieve a comprehensive understanding of service consumer needs and priorities.

Customers collaborating with each other to create a shared understanding of their business issues.

Communication for improvement

For each stakeholder group, it's important to define the **most effective methods to use**.

> *For example,*
> *the contribution to improvement from customers of a public cloud service may be through a survey or checklist of options for different functionality. For an internal customer group, the contribution to improvement may come from feedback solicited via a workshop or a collaboration tool on the organization's intranet.*

Some contributors may need to be involved at a very **detailed level**, while **others** can simply be involved as **reviewers or approvers**.

Depending on the service and the relationship between the service provider and the service consumer, the expectations about the level and type of collaboration can **vary significantly**.

Increasing urgency through visibility

When stakeholders (whether internal or external) **have poor visibility** of the workload and progression of work, the **impression is that the work is not a priority**.

Equally, when staff members attempt business-as-usual (BAU), **improvement work may seem to be a low priority** without support by the organization's management. **Insufficient visibility** of work leads to poor decision-making. To avoid this, the organization needs to:
- ✓ understanding the flow of work in progress
- ✓ identifying bottlenecks, as well as excess capacity
- ✓ uncovering waste.

*It is important to involve and address the needs of stakeholders at all levels. How it relates to the stated **vision, mission, goals and objectives** of the organization. Determining the **type**, **method** and **frequency** of such **messaging** is one of the central activities in communication.*

Applying the principle

Collaboration does not mean consensus
It is not necessary. Some organizations are so concerned with getting consensus that they try to make everyone happy and end up either doing nothing or producing something that does not properly suit anyone's needs.

Communicate in a way the audience can understand
Selecting the right method and message for each audience is critical for success.

Decisions can only be made on visible data
Making decisions in the absence of data is risky. There may be a cost to collecting data, and the organization must balance that cost against the benefit and intended usage of the data.

Think and work holistically

No service, practice, process, department or supplier stands alone
The outputs that the organization delivers to itself, customers and other stakeholders will suffer unless it works in an integrated way to handle its activities as whole, rather than as separate parts. All the organization's activities should be focused on the delivery of value.

Services are delivered to internal and external service consumers through the coordination and integration of **the four dimensions of service management.** Taking a holistic approach to service management includes establishing an understanding of how all the parts of an organization work together in an integrated way. It requires end-to-end visibility of how demand is captured and translated into outcomes.

In a complex system, the alteration of **one element can impact others** and, where possible, these impacts need to be identified, analyzed and planned for.

Applying the principle

Recognize the complexity of the systems. Different levels of complexity require different heuristics for decision-making. Applying methods and rules designed for a simple system can be ineffective or even harmful in a complex system.

Collaboration is key to thinking and working holistically If the right mechanisms are put in place for all relevant stakeholders to collaborate in a timely manner.

Look for patterns in the needs of and interactions between system elements to identify what is essential for success. With this information, needs can be anticipated, standards can be set and a holistic view point can be achieved.

Automation can support end-to-end visibility for the organization and provide an efficient means of integrated management.

Keep it simple and practical

Always use the **minimum number of steps** needed to accomplish an objective. Outcome based thinking should be used to produce **practical solutions** that deliver **valuable outcomes**.

If a process, service, action or metric provides **no value** or produces no useful outcome, then **eliminate it**.

Although this principle may seem obvious, it is **frequently ignored**.
When creating a process or a service, designers need to **think about exceptions**, but they cannot cover them all. Instead, rules should be designed that can be used to **handle exceptions generally**.

Conflicting objectives

When designing, managing, or operating practices, be mindful of **conflicting objectives.**

For example,
The management of an organization may want to collect a large amount of data to make decisions, whereas the people who must do the record-keeping may want a simpler process that does not require as much data entry.

Through the application of this, and the other guiding principles, the organization should agree on a **balance between its competing objectives**.

This example,
Services should only generate data that will truly provide value to the decision-making process, and record keeping should be simplified and automated where possible to maximize value and reduce nonvalue-adding work.

Applying the principle

Advice to keep it simple and practical:
- **Ensure value** - Every activity should contribute to the creation of value.
- **Simplicity is the ultimate sophistication**
- **Do fewer things, but do them better** - Minimizing activities to only include those with value for one or more stakeholders more focus on the quality of those actions.
- **Respect the time of the people involved** - A process that is too complicated and bureaucratic is a poor use of the time of the people involved.
- **Easier to understand, more likely to adopt** - To embed a practice, easy to follow.
- **Simplicity is the best route to achieving quick wins** - Whether in a project, or when improving daily operations activities, quick wins allow organizations to demonstrate progress and manage stakeholder expectations. Working in an iterative way with feedback will quickly deliver incremental value at regular intervals.

Optimize and automate

Organizations must **maximize** the **value** of the **work** carried out by its human and technical resources.

The **four dimensions model** provides a holistic view of the various constraints, resource types, and other areas that should be considered when designing, managing, or operating an organization.

Technology can help organizations to scale up, However, **technology should not always be relied upon** without the capability of **human intervention.**

Before it can be **effectively automated**, activities should be **optimized**. To optimize means to make something as effective and useful as it needs to be, within a set of constraints.

The road to optimization

The practices of continual improvement and **measurement** and **reporting**, are **essential** to this effort. Improve and optimize performance may draw upon **guidance from** ITIL, Lean, DevOps, Kanban and other sources. Regardless of the specific techniques, the **path** to optimization follows these **high-level steps**:

1. Understanding and agreeing the context and the overall vision and objectives of the organization.
2. Assessing the current state to understand where it can be improved and which likely to produce the biggest positive impact.
3. Agreeing what the future state and priorities should be, focusing on simplification and value. This typically also includes standardization of practices and services, which will make it easier to automate or optimize further at a later point.
4. Ensuring the optimization has the appropriate level of stakeholder engagement and commitment.
5. Executing the improvements in an iterative way, using metrics and other feedback to check progress.
6. Continually monitoring the impact of optimization to identify opportunities to improve methods of working.

Using automation

Automation typically refers to the **use of technology** to perform a step or series of steps correctly and consistently with limited or no human intervention.

For example, in organizations adopting **continuous deployment**, through to **live**, and often **automatic testing** occurring in each environment.

In its simplest form, however, automation could also mean the standardization and stream-lining of **manual tasks**. Efficiency can be greatly increased by **reducing** the need for **human involvement** to stop and evaluate each part of a process.

Opportunities for automation can be found across the entire organization to automate **standard** and **repeating tasks** can help save the organization **costs**, reduce human **error**, and improve employee **experience**

Applying the principle

Simplify and/or optimize before automating
- ✓ Take time to map out the standard and repeating processes as best as possible, and streamline where possible (optimize). From there you can start to automate.

Define your metrics
- ✓ Use the same metrics to define the baseline and to measure the achievements. Make sure that the metrics are outcome based and focused on value.

Use the other guiding principles when applying this one
- ✓ **Progress iteratively with feedback** Iterative optimization and automation make progress visible and increase stakeholder buy-in.
- ✓ **Keep it simple and practical** Things can be simple, but not optimized, so use the principles together.
- ✓ **Focusing on value** Selecting what to optimize and automate and how should be based on best value.
- ✓ **Start where you are** Make use of what is already there, but untapped or underutilized, to implement opportunities for optimization and automation quickly and economically.

Summary

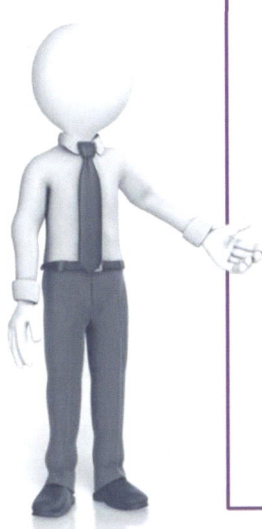

We have just talked about:

- This section has covered the ITIL guiding principles and how they can be used in all circumstances, regardless of changes in goals, strategies, type of work, or management structure. A guiding principle is universal and enduring.
- The ITIL guiding principles are:
    - *Focus on value*
    - *Start where you are*
    - *Progress iteratively with feedback*
    - *Collaborate and promote visibility*
    - *Think and work holistically*
    - *Keep it simple and practical*
    - *Optimize and automate*
- All principles integrate and can and should be used in conjunction with other available frameworks or best practices like e.g. Agile, DevOps, COBIT or Lean.

Which describes the nature of the guiding principles?

A. A guiding principle can guide an organization in all circumstances

B. Each guiding principle mandates specific actions and decisions

C. An organization will select one of the principles to adopt

D. Guiding principles describe the processes that all organizations must adopt

Which is a key consideration for the guiding principle 'keep it simple and practical'?

A. Try to create a solution for every exception

B. Understand how each element contributes to value creation

C. Ignore conflicting objectives of different stakeholders

D. Start with a complex solution, then simplify

Which guiding principle recommends organizing work into smaller, manageable sections that can be executed and completed in a timely manner?

A. Focus on value

B. Start where you are

C. Progress iteratively with feedback

D. Collaborate and promote visibility

What is the first step of the guiding principle 'focus on value'?

A. Identify the outcomes that the service facilitates

B. Identify all suppliers and partners that are involved in the service

C. Determine who the service consumer is in each situation

D. Determine the cost of provisioning the service

Course schedule
- ✓ Day 1: Key concepts of service management
  - ✓ Value creation, outcomes, costs and risks
  - ✓ Services and service relationships
  - ✓ The four dimensions
  - ✓ The ITIL service value system
  - ✓ The activities of the service value chain
  - ✓ The nature and use of the guiding principles
- • Day 2: Selected ITIL practices and key terms
  - • Service management practices
  - • General practices
  - • Technical practices

SERVICE MANAGEMENT PRACTICES

Know and understand ITIL management practices

ITIL management practices

General management practices	Service management practices	Technical management practices
Architecture management	Availability management	Deployment management
Continual improvement	Business analysis	Infrastructure and platform management
Information security management	Capacity and performance management	Software development and management
Knowledge management	**Change control**	
Measurement and reporting	**Incident management**	
Organizational change management	IT asset management	
Portfolio management	Monitoring and event management	
Project management	**Problem management**	
Relationship management	Release management	
Risk management	Service catalogue management	
Service financial management	Service configuration management	
Strategy management	Service continuity management	
Supplier management	Service design	
Workforce and talent management	**Service desk**	
	Service level management	
	Service request management	
	Service validation and testing	

IT asset management

Purpose
To plan and manage the full lifecycle of all IT assets, to help the organization:
- ✓ maximize value
- ✓ control costs
- ✓ manage risks
- ✓ support decision-making about purchase, re-use, and retirement of assets
- ✓ meet regulatory and contractual requirements.

Definition: IT asset
Any financially valuable component that can contribute to the delivery of an IT product or service.

Monitoring and event management

Purpose
To systematically observe services and service components, and record and report selected changes of state identified as events. This practice identifies and prioritizes infrastructure, services, business processes, and information security events, and establishes the appropriate response to those events, including responding to conditions that could lead to potential faults or incidents.

Definition: Event
Any change of state that has significance for the management of a service or other configuration item (CI). Events are typically recognized through notifications created by an IT service, CI, or monitoring tool.

Release management

Purpose

The purpose of the release management practice is to make new and changed services and features available for use.

Definition: Release

A version of a service or other configuration item, or a collection of configuration items, that is made available for use.

Release management in different environments

1. Release management in a traditional/waterfall environment

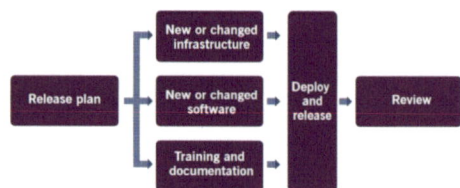

2. Release management in an Agile/DevOps environment

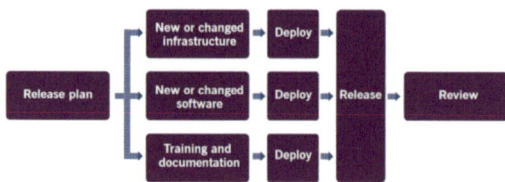

Service configuration management

Purpose

To ensure that accurate and reliable information about the configuration of services, and the CIs that support them, is available when and where it is needed.

This includes information on how CIs are configured and the relationships between them.

Definition: Configuration item
Any component that needs to be managed in order to deliver an IT service.

Change enablement

Purpose

To maximize the number of successful IT changes by ensuring that risks have been properly assessed, authorizing changes to proceed, and managing the change schedule.

Definition: Change
The addition, modification, or removal of anything that could have a direct or indirect effect on services.

Scope

The scope of change enablement is defined by each organization. It will typically include all IT infrastructure, applications, documentation, processes, supplier relationships, and anything else that might directly or indirectly impact a product or service.

Change enablement must balance the need to make beneficial changes that will deliver additional value with the need to protect customers and users from the adverse effect of changes.

It is important to distinguish change enablement from organizational change management!
- ✓ **Organizational change management:** manages the people aspects of changes to ensure that improvements and organizational transformation initiatives are implemented successfully.
- ✓ **Change enablement:** is usually focused on changes in products and services.

Three types of change

- ✓ Standard changes
  - Low-risk, pre-authorized changes that are well understood and fully documented, and can be implemented without needing additional authorization.
- ✓ Normal changes
  - Changes that need to be scheduled, assessed, and authorized following a standard process. Change models based on the type of change determine the roles for assessment and authorization. Initiation of a normal change is triggered by the creation of a change request.
- ✓ Emergency changes
  - Changes that must be implemented as soon as possible. Emergency changes are not typically included in a change schedule, and the process for assessment and authorization is expedited to ensure they can be implemented quickly.

Change authority

- ✓ **All changes** should be **assessed** by people who are able to **understand** the **risks** and the expected **benefits**; the changes must then be **authorized before** they are **deployed**.
- ✓ The person or group who authorizes a change is known as a **change authority**.
- ✓ It is essential that the correct change authority is **assigned to each type of change** to ensure that change enablement is both efficient and effective.

Change schedule

The change schedule is **used to** help **plan** changes, **assist in communication**, **avoid conflicts**, and **assign resources**. It can also be used after changes have been deployed to **provide information** needed for incident management, problem management, and improvement planning.

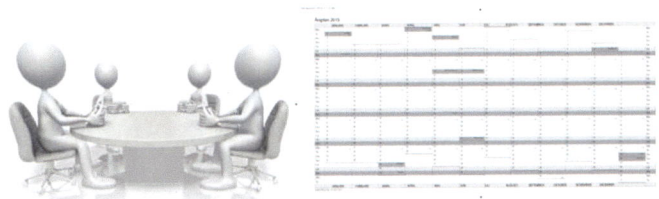

Incident management

Purpose
To minimize the negative impact of incidents by restoring normal service operation as quickly as possible.

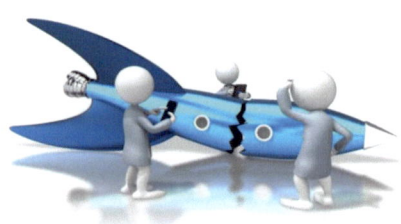

Definition: Incident
An unplanned interruption to a service or reduction in the quality of a service.

Incident management process

- ✓ There should be a formal process for logging and managing incidents.
    - This process does not usually include detailed procedures for how to diagnose, investigate, and resolve incidents, but can provide techniques for making investigation and diagnosis more efficient.
    - There may be scripts for collecting information from users during initial contact, and this may lead directly to diagnosis and resolution of simple incidents.
    - Investigation of more complicated incidents often requires knowledge and expertise, rather than procedural steps.
    - There are usually separate processes for managing major incidents, and for managing information security incidents.

- ✓ Organizations should design their incident management practice to provide appropriate management and resource allocation to different types of incident.
    - Incidents with a low impact must be managed efficiently to ensure that they do not consume too many resources.
    - Incidents with a larger impact may require more resources and more complex management.

Who can resolve incidents?

Incidents may be diagnosed and resolved by people in many different groups, depending on the complexity of the issue or the incident type:
- ✓ Some incidents will be resolved by the users themselves, using self-help.
  - Use of specific self-help records should be captured for use in measurement and improvement activities.
- ✓ Some incidents will be resolved by the service desk.
- ✓ More complex incidents will usually be escalated to a support team for resolution.
  - Typically, the routing is based on the incident category, which should help to identify the correct team.
- ✓ Incidents can be escalated to suppliers or partners, who offer support for the products and services they supply.
- ✓ The most complex incidents, and all major incidents, often require a temporary team to work together to identify the resolution.
  - This team may include representatives of many stakeholders, including the service provider, suppliers, users, etc.
- ✓ In some extreme cases, disaster recovery plans may be invoked to resolve an incident.

IT Service management tool

- ✓ Information about incidents should be stored in incident records in a suitable tool.
- ✓ It is important that people working on an incident provide good-quality updates in a timely fashion.

Impact on business

Incident management can have an enormous impact on customer and user satisfaction, and on how customers and users perceive the service provider.

- ✓ Every incident should be logged and managed to ensure that it is resolved in a time that meets the expectations of the customer and user.
- ✓ Target resolution times are agreed, documented, and communicated to ensure that expectations are realistic.
- ✓ Incidents are prioritized based on an agreed classification to ensure that incidents with the highest business impact are resolved first.

Problem management

Purpose
To reduce the likelihood and impact of incidents by identifying actual and potential causes of incidents, and managing workarounds and known errors.

Definition: Problem
A cause or potential cause of prior, current, or future incidents.

Definition: Workaround
A solution that reduces or eliminates the impact of an incident or problem for which a full resolution is not yet available. Some workarounds reduce the likelihood of incidents.

Definition: Known error
A problem that has been analysed but has not been resolved.

Problems vs. Incidents

Problems are related to incidents, but should be distinguished as they are managed in different ways:

- ✓ Incidents have an impact on users or business processes, and must be resolved so that normal business activity can take place.
- ✓ Problems are the causes of incidents. They require investigation and analysis to identify the causes, develop workarounds, and recommend longer-term resolution. This reduces the number and impact of future incidents.

The three phases of problem management

Note
Many problem management activities rely on the knowledge and experience of staff, rather than on following detailed procedures. People responsible for diagnosing problems often need the ability to understand complex systems, and to think about how different failures might have occurred.

Problem identification

Problem identification activities identify and log problems. These include:

- ✓ performing trend analysis of incident records
- ✓ detection of duplicate and recurring issues by users, service desk, and technical support staff
- ✓ during major incident management, identifying a risk that an incident could recur
- ✓ analyzing information received from suppliers and partners
- ✓ analyzing information received from internal software developers, test teams, and project teams.

Other sources of information can also lead to problems being identified.

Problem control

Problem control activities include:

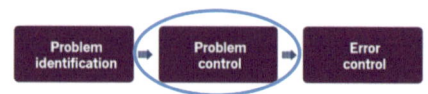

- ✓ Problem analysis
  - Problems are prioritized for analysis based on the risk that they pose, and are managed as risks based on their potential impact and probability.
  - It is not essential to analyze every problem; it is more valuable to make significant progress on the highest-priority problems than to investigate every minor problem that the organization is aware of.
- ✓ Documenting workarounds
- ✓ Documenting known errors.

Workarounds

When a problem cannot be resolved quickly, it is often useful to find and document a workaround for future incidents, based on an understanding of the problem.

- ✓ Workarounds are documented in problem records. This can be done at any stage; it doesn't need to wait for analysis to be complete.
- ✓ If a workaround has been documented early in problem control, then this should be reviewed and improved after problem analysis has been completed.

An effective incident workaround can become a permanent way of dealing with some problems when resolving the problem is not viable or cost-effective.

- ✓ In this case, the problem remains in the known error status, and the documented workaround is applied should related incidents occur.
- ✓ Every documented workaround should include a clear definition of the symptoms to which it applies.
- ✓ In some cases, workaround application can be automated.

Error control

Error control activities include:
- ✓ managing known errors, which are problems where initial analysis has been completed;
    - it usually means that faulty components have been identified.
- ✓ identification of potential permanent solutions which may result in a change request for implementation of a solution
    - but only if this can be justified in terms of cost, risks, and benefits.
- ✓ regularly re-assessing the status of known errors that have not been resolved, including overall impact on customers, availability and cost of permanent resolutions, and effectiveness of workarounds.
    - The effectiveness of workarounds should be evaluated each time a workaround is used, as the workaround may be improved based on the assessment.

Interface with other practices

Examples of interfaces between problem management, risk management, change enablement, knowledge management, and continual improvement are as follows:
- ✓ Problem management activities can be organized as a specific case of risk management
- ✓ Implementation of problem resolution is often outside the scope of problem management
- ✓ Output from the problem management practice includes information and documentation concerning workarounds and known errors
- ✓ Problem management activities can identify improvement opportunities in all four dimensions.

Service desk

Purpose

To capture demand for incident resolution and service requests. It should also be the entry point and single point of contact for the service provider with all of its users.

Value of the Service desk

- ✓ Provides a clear path for users to report issues, queries, and requests, and have them acknowledged, classified, owned, and actioned.
- ✓ With increased automation and the gradual removal of technical debt, the focus of the service desk is to provide support for 'people and business' rather than simply technical issues.
- ✓ No matter how efficient the service desk and its people are, there will always be issues that need escalation and underpinning support from other teams.
- ✓ It plays a vital role in the delivery of services, and must be actively supported by its peer groups. It is also essential to understand that the service desk '
- ✓ Has a major influence on user experience and how the service provider is perceived by the users.
- ✓ Add value not simply through the transactional acts, i.e. incident logging, but also by understanding and acting on the business context of this action.

Service desk channels

Service desks provide a variety of channels for access. These include:
- ✓ phone calls, which can include specialized technology, such as interactive voice response (IVR), conference calls, voice recognition, and others
- ✓ service portals and mobile applications, supported by service and request catalogues, and knowledge bases
- ✓ chat, through live chat and chatbots
- ✓ email for logging and updating, and for follow-up surveys and confirmations.
- ✓ walk-in service desks
- ✓ text and social media messaging
- ✓ public and corporate social media and discussion forums for contacting the service provider and for peer-to-peer support.

With increased automation, AI, and chatbots, etc. service desks are moving to provide more self-service logging and resolution. This reduces phone contact and minimize low-level work enabling the service desk to focus on excellent CX when personal contact is needed.

Service desk structures

The service desk could be:
- ✓ **centralized** e.g. a tangible team, working in a single location or
- ✓ **virtualized** allowing agents to work from multiple locations, geographically dispersed.

A virtualized service desk requires a more sophisticated supporting technology, involving more complex routing and escalation.

The service desk should be the empathetic and informed link between the service provider and its users.

Service desk staff

Service desk staff require training and competency across a number of broad technical and business areas. In particular, they need to demonstrate:
- ✓ excellent customer service skills such as empathy,
- ✓ incident analysis and prioritization,
- ✓ effective communication, and
- ✓ emotional intelligence.

The key skills for service desk staff
To be able to fully understand and diagnose a specific incident in terms of business priority, and to take appropriate action to get this resolved, using available skills, knowledge, people, and processes.

Service level management

Purpose

To set clear business-based targets for service performance, so that the delivery of a service can be properly assessed, monitored, and managed against these targets.

Definition: Service level agreement (SLA)
A documented agreement between a service provider and a customer that identifies, both services required and the expected level of service.

Service level management activities

- ✓ This practice involves the definition, documentation, and active management of service levels.
- ✓ Service level management provides the end-to-end visibility of the organization's services. To achieve this, service level management:
    - establishes a shared view of the services and target service levels with customers
    - ensures the organization meets the defined service levels through the collection, analysis, storage, and reporting of the relevant metrics for the identified services
    - performs service reviews to ensure that the current set of services continues to meet the needs of the organization and its customers
    - captures and reports on service issues, including performance against defined service levels.

Skillset needed for SLM

The skills and competencies for service level management include:
- ✓ relationship management,
- ✓ business liaison,
- ✓ business analysis,
- ✓ and commercial/supplier management.

The practice requires pragmatic focus on the whole service and not simply on its constituent parts. Simple individual metrics (such as percentage of system availability) should not be taken to represent the whole service.

Sources of information

Service level management involves collating and analyzing information from a number of sources, including:
- ✓ Customer engagement
    - This involves initial listening, discovery, and information capture on which to base metrics, measurement, and ongoing progress discussions.
- ✓ Customer feedback, ideally gathered from a number of sources, both formal and informal, including:
    - Surveys
    - Key business-related measures which are measures agreed between the service provider and its customer, based on what the customer values as important.
- ✓ Operational metrics
    - Low-level indicators of various operational activities and may include system availability, incident response and fix times, change and request processing times, and system response times.
- ✓ Business metrics
    - Can be any business activity that is deemed useful or valuable by the customer and used as a means of gauging the success of the service.

Key requirements for SLAs

They must be related to a defined 'service' in the service catalogue
- ✓ Otherwise they are simply individual metrics without a purpose, that do not provide adequate visibility or reflect the service perspective

They should relate to defined outcomes and not simply operational metrics
- ✓ This can be achieved with balanced bundles of metrics, such as customer satisfaction and key business outcomes

They should reflect an 'agreement', i.e. engagement and discussion between the service provider and the service consumer
- ✓ It's important to involve all stakeholders, including partners, sponsors, users, and customers

They must be simply written and easy to understand and use for all parties

They should not use a single-system-based metrics
- ✓ as targets can result in misalignment and a disconnect between service partners regarding the success of the service delivery and the user experience.

Service request management

Purpose

To support the agreed quality of a service by handling all pre-defined, user-initiated service requests in an effective and user-friendly manner.

> **Definition: Service request**
>
> A request from a user or a user's authorized representative that initiates a service action which has been agreed as a normal part of service delivery.

Different kind of service requests

Each service request may include one or more of the following:
- ✓ a request for a service delivery action
  - e.g. providing a report or replacing a toner cartridge
- ✓ a request for information
  - e.g. how to create a document or what the hours of the office are
- ✓ a request for provision of a resource or service
  - e.g. providing a phone or laptop to a user, or providing a virtual server for a development team
- ✓ a request for access to a resource or service
  - e.g. providing access to a file or folder
- ✓ feedback, compliments, and complaints
  - e.g. complaints about a new interface or compliments to a support team

Service request fulfilment

- ✓ Fulfilment of service requests may include changes to services or their components; usually these are standard changes.
- ✓ Service requests are a normal part of service delivery and are not a failure or degradation of service, which are handled as incidents.
- ✓ Service requests should be pre-defined and pre-agreed
  - they can usually be formalized, with a clear, standard procedure for initiation, approval, fulfilment, and management.
- ✓ The steps to fulfil the request should be well-known and proven allowing the service provider to agree times for fulfilment and provide clear communication to the users. Service requests may:
  - have very simple workflows, such as a request for information. '
  - be quite complex and require contributions from many teams and systems for fulfilment, e.g. the setup of new employee
  - be completely fulfilled by automation from submission to closure, allowing for a complete self-service experience e.g. client software installation or provision of virtual servers.

Service request authorization

Some service requests require authorization according to financial, information security, or other policies, while others may not need any. To be handled successfully, service request management should follow these guidelines:

- ✓ Service requests and their fulfilment should be standardized and automated to the greatest degree possible.
- ✓ Policies should be established regarding what service requests will be fulfilled with limited or even no additional approvals so that fulfilment can be streamlined.
- ✓ The expectations of users regarding fulfilment times should be clearly set, based on what the organization can realistically deliver.
- ✓ Opportunities for improvement should be identified and implemented to produce faster fulfilment times and take advantage of automation.
- ✓ Policies and workflows should be included for the documenting and redirecting of any requests that are submitted as service requests, but which should actually be managed as incidents or changes.

Summary

We have just talked about:

- ✓ This section has covered the service management practices that have been developed in service management and ITSM industries.
- ✓ The ITIL service management practices are:
  - *Availability management*
  - *Business analysis*
  - *Capacity and performance management*
  - **Change enablement**
  - **Incident management**
  - *IT asset management*
  - *Monitoring and event management*
  - **Problem management**
  - *Release management*
  - *Service catalogue management*
  - *Service configuration management*
  - *Service continuity management*
  - *Service design*
  - **Service desk**
  - **Service level management**
  - **Service request management**
  - *Service validation and testing*
- ✓ All practices are important for the successful provision of services
- ✓ The practices *in bold* are described in further detail and require a deeper understanding.

Which two needs should 'change enablement' BALANCE?

1. The need to assess risk and expected benefits
2. The need to manage a change schedule
3. The need to make beneficial changes
4. The need to protect customers and users

A. 1 and 2
B. 2 and 3
C. 3 and 4
D. 1 and 4

How does categorization of incidents assist incident management?

A. It helps direct the incident to the correct support area

B. It determines the priority assigned to the incident

C. It ensures that incidents are resolved in times agreed with the customer

D. It determines how the service provider is perceived

Which is NOT usually included as part of 'incident management'?

A. Scripts for collecting initial information about incidents

B. Formalized processes for logging incidents

C. Detailed procedures for the diagnosis of incidents

D. Use of specialized knowledge for complicated incidents

What should be included in every service level agreement?

A. Details of the system-based metrics used

B. A technical description of the service components

C. Clearly defined service outcomes

D. Legal language

Course schedule

- ✓ Day 1: Key concepts of service management
  - ✓ Value creation, outcomes, costs and risks
  - ✓ Services and service relationships
  - ✓ The four dimensions
  - ✓ The ITIL service value system
  - ✓ The activities of the service value chain
  - ✓ The nature and use of the guiding principles
- Day 2: Selected ITIL practices and key terms
  - ✓ Service management practices
  - General practices
  - Technical practices

GENERAL AND TECHNICAL MANAGEMENT PRACTICES

Know and understand ITIL management practices

ITIL management practices

General management practices	Service management practices	Technical management practices
Architecture management	Availability management	Deployment management
Continual improvement	Business analysis	Infrastructure and platform management
Information security management	Capacity and performance management	Software development and management
Knowledge management	**Change enablement**	
Measurement and reporting	**Incident management**	
Organizational change management	IT asset management	
Portfolio management	Monitoring and event management	
Project management	**Problem management**	
Relationship management	Release management	
Risk management	Service catalogue management	
Service financial management	Service configuration management	
Strategy management	Service continuity management	
Supplier management	Service design	
Workforce and talent management	**Service desk**	
	Service level management	
	Service request management	
	Service validation and testing	

Information security management

Purpose

To protect the information needed by the organization to conduct its business.

This includes understanding and managing risks to the **confidentiality**, **integrity**, and **availability** of information, as well as other aspects of information security such as **authentication** (ensuring someone is who they claim to be) and **non-repudiation** (ensuring that someone can't deny that they took an action).

Relationship management

Purpose

To establish and nurture the links between the organization and its stakeholders at strategic and tactical levels. It includes the identification, analysis, monitoring, and continual improvement of relationships with and between stakeholders.

Supplier management

Purpose

To ensure that the organization's suppliers and their performances are managed appropriately to support the seamless provision of quality products and services.

This includes creating closer, more collaborative relationships with key suppliers to uncover and realize new value and reduce the risk of failure.

Continual improvement

Purpose
To align the organization's practices and services with changing business needs through the ongoing identification and improvement of services, service components, practices, or any element involved in the efficient and effective management of products and services.

Everyone's responsibility!
It is important that the commitment to and practice of continual improvement is embedded into every fibre of the organization! If it is not, there is a real risk that daily operational concerns and major project work will eclipse continual improvement efforts.

Key activities

Key activities part of continual improvement practices include:
- encouraging continual improvement across the organization
- securing time and budget for continual improvement
- identifying and logging improvement opportunities
- assessing and prioritizing improvement opportunities
- making business cases for improvement action
- planning and implementing improvements
- measuring and evaluating improvement results
- coordinating improvement activities across the organization.

There are many methods, models, and techniques that can be employed for making improvements. Different types of improvement may call for different improvement methods.

The continual improvement model

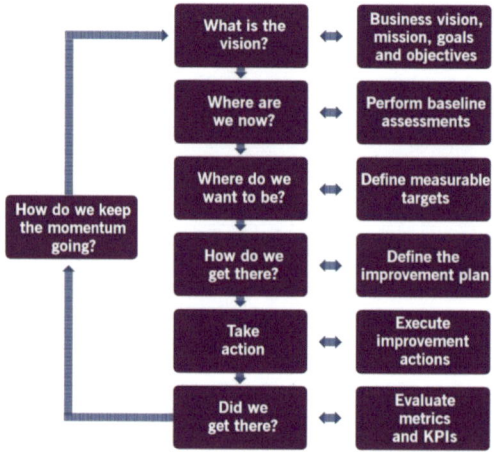

Techniques and approaches

When assessing the current state, there are many techniques that can be employed, such as a SWOT analysis, balanced scorecard reviews, internal and external assessments and audits, etc.

Organizations should develop competencies in methodologies and techniques that will meet their needs.

Approaches to continual improvement can be found in many places, e.g.:
- ✓ Lean methods provide perspectives on the elimination of waste.
- ✓ Agile methods focus on making improvement incrementally at a cadence.
- ✓ DevOps methods look at working holistically and ensuring improvements are not only designed well but applied effectively.

Focus but allow for innovation

Organizations should not try to formally commit to too many different approaches, but instead select a few key methods that are appropriate and cultivate those methods. In this way, teams will have a shared understanding of how to work together on improvements to facilitate a greater amount of change at a quicker rate.

At the same time, the organization should allow for innovation. Those in the organization with skills in alternative methods should be encouraged to apply them when it makes sense, and if this effort is successful, the alternate method may be added to the organization's repertoire. Older methods may gradually be retired in favor of new ones if better results can be achieved.

Responsibilities

Training and other enablement assistance should be provided to staff members to help them feel prepared to contribute to continual improvement.

There should be at least a small team dedicated full-time to leading continual improvement efforts and advocating for the practice across the organization. This team can serve as coordinators, guides and mentors, helping others in the organization to develop the skills they need and navigating any difficulties that may be encountered.

The highest levels of the organization need to take responsibility for embedding continual improvement into the way that people think and work. Without their leadership and visible commitment to continual improvement, attitudes, behaviour and culture will not evolve to a point where improvements are considered in everything that is done, at all levels.

Continual improvement is everyone's responsibility!

Continual improvement together with third parties

Third party suppliers should be part of the improvement effort as well.

- ✓ When contracting for a supplier's service, it is good to be sure that the contract includes details of how they will measure, report on and improve their services over the life of the contract.
- ✓ If data will be required from suppliers to operate internal improvements, that should be specified in the contract as well.

> Accurate data is the foundation of fact-based decision-making for improvement.

Continual improvement register

To track and manage improvement ideas from identification through to final action, organizations use a database or structured document called a continual improvement register (CIR).

The structure of a CIR in any given organization is not important. What is important is that improvement ideas are captured, documented, assessed, prioritized, and appropriately acted upon to ensure that the organization and its services are always being improved.

Contribution to other practices

The continual improvement practice is integral to the development and maintenance of every other practice as well as to the complete lifecycle of all services. That said, there are some practices that make a special contribution to continual improvement, i.e.:

- ✓ The organization's problem management practice can uncover issues that will be managed through continual improvement.
- ✓ The changes initiated through continual improvement may fail without the critical contributions of organizational change management.
- ✓ And many improvement initiatives will use project management practices to organize and manage their execution.

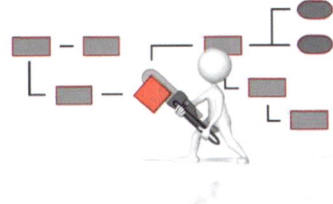

Deployment management

Purpose

To move new or changed hardware, software, documentation, processes, or any other component to live environments. It may also be involved in deploying components to other environments for testing or staging.

Summary

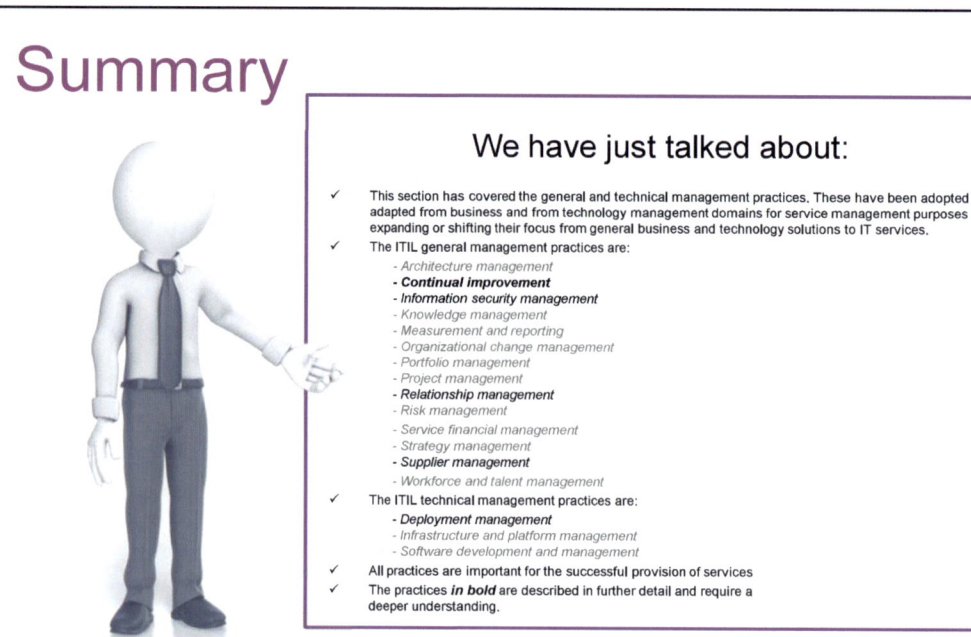

We have just talked about:

- This section has covered the general and technical management practices. These have been adopted and adapted from business and from technology management domains for service management purposes by expanding or shifting their focus from general business and technology solutions to IT services.
- The ITIL general management practices are:
  - Architecture management
  - **Continual improvement**
  - **Information security management**
  - Knowledge management
  - Measurement and reporting
  - Organizational change management
  - Portfolio management
  - Project management
  - **Relationship management**
  - Risk management
  - Service financial management
  - Strategy management
  - **Supplier management**
  - Workforce and talent management
- The ITIL technical management practices are:
  - **Deployment management**
  - Infrastructure and platform management
  - Software development and management
- All practices are important for the successful provision of services
- The practices *in bold* are described in further detail and require a deeper understanding.

A. Use a new method for each improvement that the organization handles

B. Select a few key methods to suit the types of improvement that the organization handles

C. Build the capability to use as many improvement methods as possible

D. Select a single method for all improvements that the organization handles

Which practice is responsible for moving components to live environments?

A. Change enablement

B. Release management

C. IT asset management

D. Deployment management

What is the purpose of 'supplier management'?

A. To ensure that the organization's suppliers and their performance are managed appropriately to support the provision of seamless, quality products and services

B. To align the organization's practices and services with changing business needs through the ongoing identification and improvement of services

C. To ensure that the organization's suppliers and their performance are managed appropriately at strategic and tactical levels through coordinated marketing, selling and delivery activities

D. To ensure that accurate and reliable information about the configuration of supplier's services is available when and where it is needed

Which practice is the responsibility of everyone in the organization?

A. Service level management

B. Change enablement

C. Problem management

D. Continual improvement

Course schedule

✓ Day 1: Key concepts of service management
   ✓ Value creation, outcomes, costs and risks
   ✓ Services and service relationships
   ✓ The four dimensions
   ✓ The ITIL service value system
   ✓ The activities of the service value chain
   ✓ The nature and use of the guiding principles

✓ Day 2: Selected ITIL practices and key terms
   ✓ Service management practices
   ✓ General practices
   ✓ Technical practices

Certification scheme

The ITIL 4 certification scheme that has two main training streams and three levels:

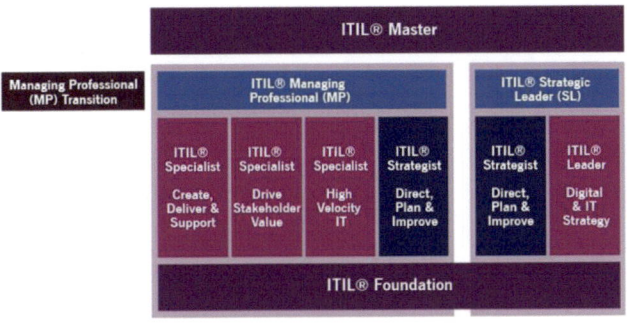

- Designation achieved once completed all relevant examinable modules in each stream
- Examinable modules towards ITIL Managing Professional and ITIL Strategic Leader
- Examinable module applicable to both ITIL Managing Professional and ITIL Strategic Leader
- Transition module for v3 ITIL Experts or those with 17 credits or more to gain ITIL Managing Professional designation

Examination preparation

The ITIL 4 Foundation exam in short:
- ✓ 40 multiple-choice questions
- ✓ Each question is worth 1 mark. There are 40 marks available
- ✓ There is no negative marking
- ✓ Pass rate is 65% or higher – a raw score of 26 marks or above
- ✓ Duration is 60 minutes (75 minutes if not native in English)
- ✓ This is a 'closed book' examination. No materials other than the examination materials are permitted.

Good luck with the exam!

Thank you!

ITIL® 4 Foundation exercises

The following exercises can be solved individually, in pairs or in teams.

1. Service management key concepts

1.1 Value

List examples of value

- What is the value? _____

- Who are the stakeholders? _____

- How is value facilitated through services? _____

  _____

  _____

1.2 Organization

Describe an "organization" in your own company

- Which people are a part of the organization? _____

- What are their responsibilities? _____

- What are their authorities/mandate? _____

- What is the objective of the organization (briefly)? _____

  _____

  _____

1.3 Stakeholders/consumers

List examples of the following stakeholders from your own organization

- Customer _____

- User _____

- Sponsor _____

- Other types of stakeholders _____

1.4 Co-creation

List examples of provisioning and consumption of services from your ovn organization:

- Which activities does the service provider perform?

  _____

  _____

- Which activities does the service consumer perform?

  _____

  _____

- Which activities are performed jointly – or COULD be performed jointly?

  _____

  _____

1.5 Service relations

Describe service relation with service offerings, goods, access to resources and service actions. Use the template below or draw on paper/flipover.

If there is spare time, also note products and resources.

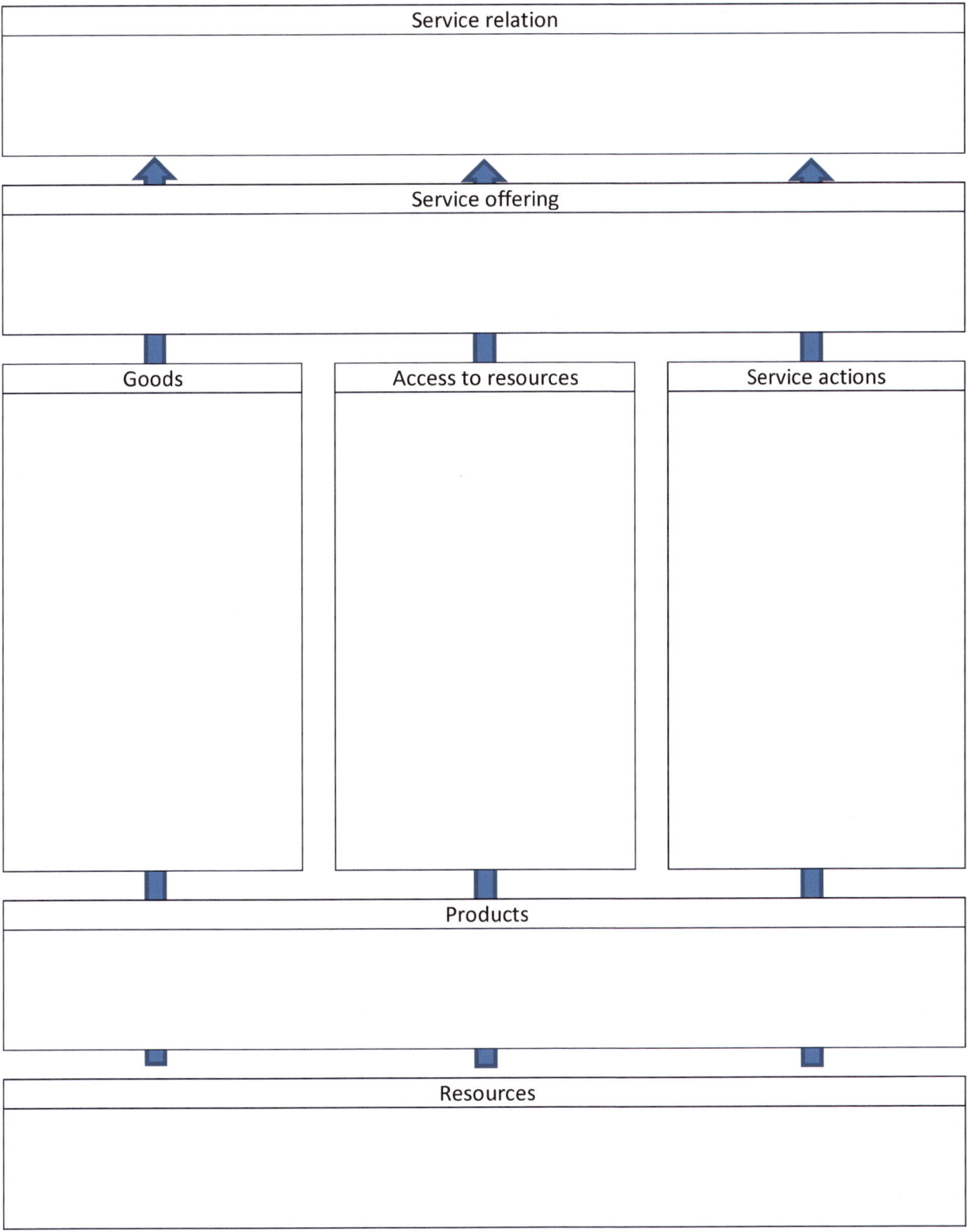

1.6 Output/outcome

List an example of output from your own organization. Describe how this output facilitates an outcome.

- Output: _____

- Resultat: _____

1.7 Costs and riscs

Describe costs and riscs in your own organization

- Costs: _____

- Riscs: _____

1.8 Utility and warranty

Using the service relation from 1.5, describe:

- The utility of the service offering: _____

- The warranty of the service offering: _____

- One example where the utility and/or warranty of the service relation does not match the promises of the service offering – or the expectations of the consumer:

  _____

2. ITIL key concepts

2.1 Organizations & people

List examples of conflicts between:

- "Communication and cooperation" and "breaking down silos": _____

  _____

- "Updating skills and competencies" and "Broad knowledge and deep specialization": ____

  _____

2.2 Information & technology

Consider a technological solution from your own organization. Evaluate the solution against the below "checklist".

Technological solution:			
	Is it compatible with the current architecture?		Does the organization have the skills in the organization to support and maintain it?
	Does it raise any regulatory, compliance or information security control issues?		Does it have sufficient automation capabilities to be developed, deployed and operated?
	Is it viable in the foreseeable future?		Does it have additional capabilities that can be used for other products or services?
	Does it align with service provider or service consumer strategy?		Does it introduce new risks or constraints to the organization?

2.3 Partners & suppliers

List partners from your own organization where the relationship is characterized by:

- Service partnership (cooperate and share common goals and riscs): _____

  _____

- Supplier of goods and services (formal contracts, clear separation of responsibilities): ___

  _____

2.4 Value streams & processes

Describe a process from your own organization:

- Input:_____

- Output:_____

- Value created by this output:_____

- Activities that convert input to output:

_____

_____

_____

_____

2.5 Siloes

Describe an example of siloes in your own organization: _____

2.6 Value chain activities

Fill in the blanks with the correct value chain activities

Planning at all levels is performed by _____

All interactions with external parties are performed by _____

Improvements are initiated and managed via _____

All new resources are obtained through _____

Creation, modification, delivery, maintenance and support of components, products and services are performed in an integrated and coordinated way between

_____,

_____ and

_____

2.7 ITIL guiding principles

Match each guiding principle with the correct application of the principle

Guiding principle
Focus on value
Start where you are
Progress iteratively with feedback
Collaborate and promote visibility
Think and work holistically
Keep it simple and practical
Optimize and automate

Application
Simplify and/or optimize before automating
Decisions can only be made on visible data
Know how consumers use each service
Collaboration is key to thinking and working holistically
The ecosystem is constantly evolving, so feedback is essential
Look at what exists as objectively as possible
Easier to understand, more likely to adopt

3. ITIL practices

3.1 Continual improvement model

Match the elements in the continual improvement model with each other

What is the vision?		Define improvement plan
Where are we now?		Baseline assessment
Where do we want to be?		
How do we get there?		Define measurable targets
Take action		Evaluate metrics and KPIs
Did we get there?		Execute the plan
How do we keep momentum?		Business vision, mission, goals and objectives

3.2 Service management practices

Describe a situation, where a user has experienced an unavailable service.

_____

_____

3.3 Capacity and performance management

Describe a situation, where a user has experienced bad service performance.

_____

_____

3.4 Change enablement

What characterizez:

- Standard changes: _____

- Normal changes: _____

- Emergency changes: _____

3.5 Incident management

List examples from your own organization how to perform the following with incidents:

- Log: _____

- Meet agreed target resolution times: _____

- Prioritize: _____

3.6 IT asset management

Describe planning and managing the lifecycle of one IT asset in your own organization.

_____ ,

_____ og

3.7 Monitoring and event management

Explain how you handle events in your own organization.

_____ ,

_____ og

3.8 Problem management

What is stored in a known error database? Mark the correct answers with an X.

Problems	
Incidents	
Problem analysis	
Events	

Changes	
Known errors	
Availability	
Workarounds	

Van Haren Publishing®

3.9 Service configuration management

Describe how service configuration management integrates with IT asset management.

_____
_____
_____

3.10 Service continuity management

Describe how your organization ensures that the availability and performance of a service is maintained at a sufficient level in the event of a disaster.

_____
_____

3.11 Service desk

List examples of service desk access channels and technologies/tools in your own organization.

Access channels	Technologies/tools

3.12 Service level management

Which parties agree on an SLA (service level agreement)?

_____ og _____

3.13 Service request management

Mark with an X the texts that describe Service request management best practice:

	Standardize and automate		Have many approval levels
	Set expectations		Have <u>one</u> process for errors/requests
	Identify improvements		If possible, fulfill requests manually
	Limit approvals		Make authorization cumbersome

3.14 Practices terms

The below table shows a list of practices and descriptions of definitions of these practices. Enter the matching term in the empty column.

#	Practice	Term	Definition description
1	Availability management		The ability of an IT service or other configuration item to perform its agreed function when required
2	Capacity and performance management		A measure of what is achieved or delivered by a system, person, team, practice or service
3	Capacity and performance management		The number of service actions performed in a timeframe, and the time required to fulfil a service action, at a given level of demand
4	Capacity and performance management		The maximum throughput that a configuration item or service can deliver
5	Change enablement		The addition, modification, or removal of anything that could have a direct or indirect effect on services
6	Change enablement		Pre-authorized Implement without further authorization
7	Change enablement		Authorization based on change type
8	Change enablement		Expedited assessment and authorization May be separate change authority
9	Change enablement		The person or group who authorizes a change
0	Change enablement		Is used to help plan changes, assist in communication, avoid conflicts and assign resources
10	Incident management		An unplanned interruption to a service, or reduction in the quality of a service
11	IT asset management		Any valuable component that can contribute to delivery of an IT product or service
12	Monitoring and event management		Any change of state that has significance for the management of a configuration item (CI) or IT service
13	Problem management		A cause or potential cause of prior, current, or future incidents.
14	Problem management		A problem that has been analyzed, but not yet resolved
15	Problem management		A solution that reduces or eliminates the impact of an incident or problem for which a full resolution is not yet available
16	Service configuration management		Any component that needs to be managed in order to deliver an IT service
17	Service continuity management		A sudden unplanned event that causes great damage or serious loss to an organization
18	Service level management		A documented agreement between a service provider and a customer that identifies serviced required and the expected level of service

| 19 | Service request management | | A request from a user or user's authorized representative that initiates a service action that has been agreed as a normal part of service delivery |

3.15 Practices purposes

The below table shows a list of purposes for different practices. Enter the correct practice name in the empty column.

#	Practice (name)	Purpose
1		To align the organization's practices and services with changing business needs through ongoing identification of improvement opportunities
2		To protect the information needed by the organization to conduct its business
3		To establish and nurture the links between the organization and its stakeholders at strategic and tactical levels
4		To ensure that the organization's suppliers and their performance are managed appropriately
5		To ensure that services deliver agreed levels of availability to meet the needs of customers and users
6		To ensure that services achieve agreed and expected performance, satisfying current and future demand in a cost-effective way
7		To maximize the number of successful IT changes by ensuring that risks have been properly assessed, authorizing changes to proceed, and managing a change schedule
8		To minimize the negative impact of incidents by restoring normal service operation as quickly as possible
9		To plan and manage the full lifecycle of all IT assets
10		To systematically observe services and service components, and record and report selected changes of state identified as events
11		To reduce the likelihood and impact of incidents by identifying actual and potential causes of incidents, and managing workarounds and known errors
12		To make new and changed services and features available for use
13		To ensure that accurate and reliable information about the configuration of services, and the CIs that support them, is available when and where needed
14		To ensure that the availability and performance of a service is maintained at a sufficient level in the event of a disaster
15		To capture demand for incident resolution and service requests. It should also be the entry point/SPOC for the service provider with all of its users
16		To set clear business-based targets for service performance, so that the delivery of a service can be properly assessed, monitored and managed against these targets
17		To support the agreed quality of a service by handling all pre-defined, user-initiated service requests in an effective and user-friendly manner

| 18 | | To move new or changed hardware, software, documentation, processes, or any other component to live environments |

4. Case – value streams and processes

Use the below example to create a simple value stream from your own organization.

Value chain activity	Practice	Roles	Activities
Demand		Admin assistant	An admin assistant in an office is unable to enter an appointment in their calendar due to a bug in the calendar application which won't allow a non-standard character to be used in a room name.
Engage	Service desk, Incident management	Admin assistant, Service desk agent	The admin assistant phones the service desk and describes the issue. The expected resolution time is agreed.. Information about this incident is logged by the service desk agent.
Deliver and support	Incident management	Service desk	The service desk agent researches the vendor website and discovers that this particular issue is resolved in the latest version of the client software.
Deliver and support	Incident management, Supplier management	Service desk agent, Second line	The incident is escalated to second line support. Second line support check the vendor contract, and the release notes for the client
Deliver and support, Obtain/ build, Engage	Incident mgt, Service request mgt, Deployment mgt, Service validation and testing	Second line support, Admin assistant	Second line support contact the user and arrange for them to test the new version of the client software to see if this resolves their issue. They then add this version to the service portal so that the user can install it.
Deliver and support	Incident management, Service validation and testing, Service request management	Admin assistant, Service desk	The user installs the new version of the software, using the service portal, and tests whether this resolves their issue. The service desk ensures that the user is satisfied with this solution.
Value		Admin assistant	The software now works correctly. The user can add appointments to the calendar using non-standard characters in room names.
Engage, Improve	Service desk, Incident management, Continual improvement	Admin assistant, Service desk manager	A brief satisfaction survey is emailed to the admin assistant, which they complete and return. The scores are used to identify trends, and the comments are passed to the service desk manager for consideration.
Improve	Continual improvement, Service validation and testing, Service request management, Release management, Deployment management	Second line support	Second line support carry out more extensive testing of the new version of the client software, and then make it available to all users via the service portal. The upgrade to replace the previous version is then deployed in a controlled way.

The ITIL® 4 Foundation Examination

Sample Paper 1

Question Booklet

Multiple Choice

Examination Duration: 1 Hour

Instructions

1. You should attempt all 40 questions. Each question is worth one mark.
2. There is only one correct answer per question.
3. You need to answer 26 questions correctly to pass the exam.
4. Mark your answers on the answer sheet provided. Use a pencil (NOT pen).
5. You have 60 minutes to complete this exam.
6. This is a 'closed book' exam. No material other than the exam paper is allowed.

The ITIL® 4 Foundation Examination

1) Which practice is responsible for moving components to live environments?

   A. Change enablement
   B. Release management
   C. IT asset management
   D. Deployment management

2) Which practice includes the classification and ownership of queries and requests from users?

   A. Service desk
   B. Incident management
   C. Change enablement
   D. Service level management

3) Which practice identifies metrics that reflect the **customer's** experience of a service?

   A. Continual improvement
   B. Service desk
   C. Service level management
   D. Problem management

4) What is the PRIMARY use of a change schedule?

   A. To support 'incident management' and improvement planning
   B. To manage emergency changes
   C. To plan changes and help avoid conflicts
   D. To manage standard changes

5) Which service management dimension is focused on activities and how these are coordinated?

   A. Organizations and people
   B. Information and technology
   C. Partners and suppliers
   D. Value streams and processes

The ITIL® 4 Foundation Examination

6) How does categorization of incidents assist the 'incident management' practice?

    A. It helps direct the incident to the correct support area
    B. It determines the priority assigned to the incident
    C. It ensures that incidents are resolved in timescales agreed with the customer
    D. It determines how the service provider is perceived

7) Identify the missing word(s) in the following sentence.

    A service is a means of enabling value co-creation by facilitating [?] that customers want to achieve.

    A. the warranty
    B. outcomes
    C. the utility
    D. outputs

8) Which is a recommendation of the 'continual improvement' practice?

    A. There should at least be a small team dedicated to leading 'continual improvement' efforts
    B. All improvements should be managed as multi-phase projects
    C. 'Continual improvement' should be isolated from other practices
    D. External suppliers should be excluded from improvement initiatives

9) Which is a potential benefit of using an IT service management tool to support the 'incident management' practice?

    A. It may ensure that the cause of incidents is identified within agreed times
    B. It may provide automated matching of incidents to problems or known errors
    C. It may ensure that supplier contracts are aligned with the needs of the service provider
    D. It may provide automated resolution and closure of complex incidents

10) Which role submits service requests?

   A. The user, or their authorized representative
   B. The customer, or their authorized representative
   C. The sponsor, or their authorized representative
   D. The supplier, or their authorized representative

11) Which practice provides a single point of contact for users?

   A. Incident management
   B. Change enablement
   C. Service desk
   D. Service request management

12) Which guiding principle recommends that the four dimensions of service management are considered?

   A. Think and work holistically
   B. Progress iteratively with feedback
   C. Focus on value
   D. Keep it simple and practical

13) Which would be supported by the 'service request management' practice?

   A. A request to authorize a change that could have an effect on a service
   B. A request from a user for something which is a normal part of service delivery
   C. A request to restore service after a service interruption
   D. A request to investigate the cause of multiple related incidents

14) Which practice is the responsibility of everyone in the organization?

   A. Service level management
   B. Change enablement
   C. Problem management
   D. Continual improvement

15) Identify the missing word in the following sentence.

The purpose of the 'information security management' practice is to [?] the organization's information.

   A. store
   B. provide
   C. audit
   D. protect

16) Which guiding principle recommends collecting data before deciding what can be re-used?

   A. Focus on value
   B. Start where you are
   C. Keep it simple and practical
   D. Progress iteratively with feedback

17) Which is NOT usually included as part of incident management?

   A. Scripts for collecting initial information about incidents
   B. Formalized procedures for logging incidents
   C. Detailed procedures for the diagnosis of incidents
   D. The use of specialized knowledge for complicated incidents

18) Which describes the nature of the guiding principles?

   A. Guiding principles can guide an organization in all circumstances
   B. Each guiding principle mandates specific actions and decisions
   C. An organization will select and adopt only one of the seven guiding principles
   D. Guiding principles describe the processes that all organizations must adopt

19) Which statement about a change authority is CORRECT?

   A. A single change authority should be assigned to authorize all types of change and change models
   B. A change authority should be assigned for each type of change and change model
   C. Normal changes are pre-authorized and do not need a change authority
   D. Emergency changes can be implemented without authorization from a change authority

20) Which practice has the purpose of making new and changed services and features available for use?

   A. Change enablement
   B. Service request management
   C. Release management
   D. Deployment management

21) Which value chain activity ensures people understand the organization's vision?

   A. Improve
   B. Plan
   C. Deliver and support
   D. Obtain/build

22) Which statement about the value chain activities is CORRECT?

   A. Every practice belongs to a specific value chain activity
   B. A specific combination of value chain activities and practices forms a service relationship
   C. Service value chain activities form a single workflow that enables value creation
   D. Each value chain activity contributes to the value chain by transforming specific inputs into outputs

23) What is the purpose of the 'supplier management' practice?

   A. To ensure that the organization's suppliers and their performance are managed appropriately to support the seamless provision of quality products and services
   B. To align the organization's practices and services with changing business needs through the ongoing identification and improvement of services
   C. To ensure that the organization's suppliers and their performance are managed appropriately at strategic and tactical levels through coordinated marketing, selling, and delivery activities
   D. To ensure that accurate and reliable information about the configuration of suppliers' services is available when and where it is needed

24) What are the two types of cost that a service consumer should evaluate?

   A. The price of the service, and the cost of creating the service
   B. The costs removed by the service, and the costs imposed by the service
   C. The cost of provisioning the service, and the cost of improving the service
   D. The cost of software, and the cost of hardware

25) Which is a purpose of the 'service desk' practice?

   A. To reduce the likelihood and impact of incidents by identifying actual and potential causes of incidents
   B. To maximize the number of successful IT changes by ensuring risks are properly assessed
   C. To capture demand for incident resolution and service requests
   D. To set clear business-based targets for service performance

26) How should an organization adopt continual improvement methods?

   A. Use a new method for each improvement the organization handles
   B. Select a few key methods for the types of improvement that the organization handles
   C. Build the capability to use as many improvement methods as possible
   D. Select a single method for all improvements that the organization handles

27) Which ITIL concept describes governance?

   A. The seven guiding principles
   B. The four dimensions of service management
   C. The service value chain
   D. The service value system

28) Which is a recommendation of the 'service desk' practice?

   A. Service desks should avoid the use of automation
   B. Service desks should be highly technical
   C. Service desks should understand the wider organization
   D. Service desks should be a physical team in a single fixed location

29) Which guiding principle recommends organizing work into smaller, manageable sections that can be executed and completed in a timely manner?

   A. Focus on value
   B. Start where you are
   C. Progress iteratively with feedback
   D. Collaborate and promote visibility

30) What is a standard change?

   A. A change that is well understood, fully documented and pre-authorized
   B. A change that needs to be assessed, authorized, and scheduled by a change authority
   C. A change that doesn't need a risk assessment because it is required to resolve an incident
   D. A change that is assessed, authorized, and scheduled as part of 'continual improvement'

31) What happens if a workaround becomes the permanent way of dealing with a problem that cannot be resolved cost-effectively?

   A. A change request is submitted to change enablement
   B. Problem management restores the service as soon as possible
   C. The problem remains in the known error status
   D. The problem record is deleted

32) What is the definition of change?

   A. To add, modify or remove anything that could have a direct or indirect effect on services
   B. To ensure that accurate and reliable information about the configuration of services is available
   C. To make new and changed services and features available for use
   D. To move new or changed hardware, software, or any other component to live environments

33) What is the definition of an event?

   A. Any change of state that has significance for the management of a service or other configuration item
   B. Any component that needs to be managed in order to deliver an IT service
   C. An unplanned interruption to a service or reduction in the quality of a service
   D. Any financially valuable component that can contribute to the delivery of an IT product or service

34) Which describes outcomes?

   A. Tangible or intangible deliverables
   B. Functionality offered by a product or service
   C. Results desired by a stakeholder
   D. Configuration of an organization's resources

35) Which is NOT a key focus of the 'information and technology' dimension?

    A. Security and compliance
    B. Communication systems and knowledge bases
    C. Workflow management and inventory systems
    D. Roles and responsibilities

36) Which practices are typically involved in the implementation of a problem resolution?

    1. Continual improvement
    2. Service request management
    3. Service level management
    4. Change enablement

    A. 1 and 2
    B. 2 and 3
    C. 3 and 4
    D. 1 and 4

37) Which is a key consideration for the guiding principle 'keep it simple and practical'?

    A. Try to create a solution for every exception
    B. Understand how each element contributes to value creation
    C. Ignore the conflicting objectives of different stakeholders
    D. Start with a complex solution, then simplify

38) What should be done first when applying the 'focus on value' guiding principle?

    A. Identify the outcomes that the service facilitates
    B. Identify all suppliers and partners involved in the service
    C. Determine who the service consumer is in each situation
    D. Determine the cost of providing the service

39) A service provider describes a package that includes a laptop with software, licenses, and support. What is this package an example of?

   A. Value
   B. An outcome
   C. Warranty
   D. A service offering

40) What is the definition of warranty?

   A. A tangible or intangible deliverable that is produced by carrying out an activity
   B. The assurance that a product or service will meet agreed requirements
   C. A possible event that could cause harm or loss, or make it more difficult to achieve objectives
   D. The functionality offered by a product or service to meet a particular need

The ITIL® 4 Foundation Examination

Sample Paper 1

Answers and Rationales

The ITIL® 4 Foundation Examination

For exam paper: EN_ITIL4_FND_2019_SamplePaper1_QuestionBk_v1.4

Q	A	Syllabus Ref	Rationale
1	D	6.1.h	A. Incorrect. "The purpose of the change enablement practice is to maximize the number of successful service and product changes by ensuring that risks have been properly assessed, authorizing changes to proceed, and managing the change schedule". Ref 5.2.4 B. Incorrect. "The purpose of the release management practice is to make new and changed services and features available for use." Ref 5.2.9 C. Incorrect. "The purpose of the IT asset management practice is to plan and manage the full lifecycle of all IT assets". Ref 5.2.6 D. Correct. "The purpose of the deployment management practice is to move new or changed hardware, software, documentation, processes, or any other component to live environments." Ref 5.3.1
2	A	7.1.f	A. Correct. "Service desks provide a clear path for users to report issues, queries, and requests, and have them acknowledged, classified, owned, and actioned". Ref 5.2.14 B. Incorrect. The 'incident management' practice deals only with incidents, not queries and requests. "The purpose of the incident management practice is to minimize the negative impact of incidents by restoring normal service operation as quickly as possible". Ref 5.2.5 C. Incorrect. The 'change enablement' practice deals only with change requests, not other queries and requests. "The purpose of the change enablement practice is to maximize the number of successful service and product changes by ensuring that risks have been properly assessed, authorizing changes to proceed, and managing the change schedule". Ref 5.2.4 D. Incorrect. The 'service level management' practice ensures service targets are met. It does not manage queries and requests from users. "The purpose of the service level management practice is to set clear business-based targets for service performance, so that the delivery of a service can be properly assessed, monitored, and managed against these targets". Ref 5.2.15

The ITIL® 4 Foundation Examination

Q	A	Syllabus Ref	Rationale
3	C	7.1.g	A. Incorrect. "The purpose of the continual improvement practice is to align the organization's practices and services with changing business needs through the ongoing improvement of products, services, and practices, or any element involved in the management of products and services." Ref 5.1.2 B. Incorrect. "The purpose of the service desk practice is to capture demand for incident resolution and service requests. It should also be the entry point and single point of contact for the service provider with all of its users." Ref 5.2.14 C. Correct. "Service level management identifies metrics and measures that are a truthful reflection of the customer's actual experience and level of satisfaction with the whole service," and "Engagement is needed to understand and confirm the actual ongoing needs and requirements of customers, not simply what is interpreted by the service provider or has been agreed several years before." Ref 5.2.15.1 D. Incorrect. "The purpose of the problem management practice is to reduce the likelihood and impact of incidents by identifying actual and potential causes of incidents, and managing workarounds and known errors". Ref 5.2.8
4	C	7.1.b	A. Incorrect. While it can be used after deploying a change, this is not the main use of the change schedule. "The change schedule is used to help plan changes, assist in communication, avoid conflicts, and assign resources. It can also be used after changes have been deployed to provide information needed for incident management, problem management, and improvement planning." Ref 5.2.4 B. Incorrect. "Emergency changes: These are changes that must be implemented as soon as possible; for example, to resolve an incident or implement a security patch. Emergency changes are not typically included in a change schedule, and the process for assessment and authorization is expedited to ensure they can be implemented quickly." Ref 5.2.4 C. Correct. "The change schedule is used to help plan changes, assist in communication, avoid conflicts, and assign resources." Ref 5.2.4 D. Incorrect. Standard changes are already pre-authorized and do not need to be included on a change schedule. "These are low-risk, pre-authorized changes that are well understood and fully documented, and can be implemented without needing additional authorization." Ref 5.2.4

Q	A	Syllabus Ref	Rationale
5	D	3.1.d	A. Incorrect. The 'organizations and people' dimension describes "roles and responsibilities, formal organizational structures, culture, and required staffing and competencies." Ref 3.1 B. Incorrect. The 'information and technology' dimension includes "the information and knowledge necessary for the management of services, as well as the technologies required" and "the information created, managed, and used in the course of service provision and consumption, and the technologies that support and enable that service." Ref 3.2 C. Incorrect. "The partners and suppliers dimension encompasses an organization's relationships with other organizations that are involved in the design, development, deployment, delivery, support and/or continual improvement of services. It also incorporates contracts and other agreements between the organization and its partners or suppliers". Ref 3.3 D. Correct. The 'value streams and processes' dimension "focuses on what activities the organization undertakes and how they are organized, as well as how the organization ensures that it is enabling value creation for all stakeholders efficiently and effectively." Ref 3.4
6	A	7.1.c	A. Correct. "More complex incidents will usually be escalated to a support team for resolution. Typically, the routing is based on the incident category, which should help to identify the correct team." Ref 5.2.5 B. Incorrect. The category is concerned with the type of incident whereas priority is determined by business impact. "Incidents are prioritized based on agreed classification to ensure that incidents with the highest business impact are resolved first." Ref 5.2.5 C. Incorrect. "Every incident should be logged and managed to ensure that it is resolved in a time that meets the expectations of the customer and user." Categorization by itself will not ensure this. Ref 5.2.5 D. Incorrect. Customer and user satisfaction determines how the service provider is perceived. "Incident management can have an enormous impact on customer and user satisfaction, and on how customers and users perceive the service provider." Ref 5.2.5

The ITIL® 4 Foundation Examination

Q	A	Syllabus Ref	Rationale
7	B	1.1.a	A. Incorrect. Warranty is "assurance that a product or service will meet agreed requirements." Warranty of a service is necessary, but not sufficient to enable value co-creation. Ref 2.5.4 B. Correct. A service is "a means of enabling value co-creation by facilitating outcomes that customers want to achieve, without the customer having to manage specific costs and risks". Ref 2.3.1 C. Incorrect. Utility is "the functionality offered by a product or service". Utility of a service is necessary, but not sufficient to enable value co-creation. Ref 2.5.4 D. Incorrect. An output is "a tangible or intangible deliverable of an activity." The output of a service is necessary, but not sufficient to enable value co-creation. Ref 2.5.1
8	A	7.1.a	A. Correct. "Although everyone should contribute in some way, there should at least be a small team dedicated full-time to leading continual improvement efforts and advocating the practice across the organization." Ref 5.1.2 B. Incorrect. "Different types of improvements may call for different improvement methods. For example, some improvements may be best organized into a multi-phase project, while others may be more appropriate as a single quick effort." Ref 5.1.2 C. Incorrect. "The continual improvement practice is integral to the development and maintenance of every other practice." Ref 5.1.2 D. Incorrect. "When third-party suppliers form part of the service landscape, they should also be part of the improvement effort." Ref 5.1.2
9	B	7.1.c	A. Incorrect. "Target resolution times are agreed, documented, and communicated to ensure that expectations are realistic." A good IT service management tool may help the organization to meet these times, but the tool cannot ensure that this happens. Furthermore, identifying the causes of incidents is a 'problem management' activity Ref 5.2.5 B. Correct. "Modern IT service management tools can provide automated matching of incidents to other incidents, problems or known errors". Ref 5.2.5 C. Incorrect. 'Incident management' requires supplier contracts to be correctly aligned, but ensuring that the contracts are aligned is a purpose of the 'supplier management' practice. Ref 5.1.13 D. Incorrect. "The most complex incidents, and all major incidents, often require a temporary team to work together to identify the resolution". "Investigation of more complicated incidents often requires knowledge and expertise, rather than procedural steps." Ref 5.2.5

The ITIL® 4 Foundation Examination

Q	A	Syllabus Ref	Rationale
10	A	7.1.e	A. Correct. "The purpose of the service request management practice is to support the agreed quality of a service by handling all pre-defined, user-initiated service requests..." and a service request is defined as "a request from a user or a user's authorized representative that initiates a service action". Ref 5.2.16 B. Incorrect. A customer is "the role that defines the requirements for a service and takes responsibility for the outcomes of service consumption". A customer could also be a user, and in that role they may submit a service request. Ref 2.2.2 C. Incorrect. A sponsor is "the role that authorizes budget for service consumption." A sponsor could also be a user, and in that role they may submit a service request. Ref 2.2.2 D. Incorrect. "The partners and suppliers dimension encompasses an organization's relationships with other organizations that are involved in the design, development, deployment, delivery, support, and/or continual improvement of services.". This does not include consumption of services, and "The purpose of the service request management practice is to support the agreed quality of a service by handling all pre-defined, user-initiated service requests." Ref 3.3, 5.2.16
11	C	7.1.f	A. Incorrect. "The purpose of the incident management practice is to minimize the negative impact of incidents by restoring normal service operation as quickly as possible." The 'incident management' practice does not provide a single point of contact for service users. Ref 5.2.5 B. Incorrect. "The purpose of the change enablement practice is to maximize the number of successful service and product changes by ensuring that risks have been properly assessed, authorizing changes to proceed, and managing the change schedule." The 'change enablement' practice does not provide a single point of contact for service users. Ref 5.2.4 C. Correct. "The purpose of the service desk practice is to capture demand for incident resolution and service requests. It should also be the entry point and single point of contact for the service provider with all of its users." Ref 5.2.14 D. Incorrect. "The purpose of the service request management practice is to support the agreed quality of a service by handling all pre-defined, user-initiated service requests in an effective and user-friendly manner." The 'service request management' practice does not provide a single point of contact for service users. Ref 5.2.16

The ITIL® 4 Foundation Examination

Q	A	Syllabus Ref	Rationale
12	A	2.2.e	A. Correct. The 'think and work holistically' guiding principle advises that all aspects of an organization are considered when providing value in the form of services. This includes all four dimensions of service management (organizations and people; information and technology; partners and suppliers; value streams and processes). "Services are delivered to internal and external service consumers through the coordination and integration of the four dimensions of service management." Ref 4.3.5 B. Incorrect. The 'progress iteratively with feedback' guiding principle is concerned with breaking initiatives into manageable sections that can be executed more easily. It is not primarily concerned with addressing the four dimensions of service management. Ref 4.3.3 C. Incorrect. The 'focus on value' guiding principle ensures that everything that the organization does links back to providing value to service consumers. It is not primarily concerned with addressing the four dimensions of service management. Ref 4.3.1 D. Incorrect. The 'keep it simple and practical' guiding principle focuses on keeping things simple by reducing complexity and eliminating unnecessary activities and steps. It is not primarily concerned with addressing the four dimensions of service management. Ref 4.3.6
13	B	7.1.e	A. Incorrect. This would be supported by the 'change enablement' practice. A change is "the addition, modification, or removal of anything that could have a direct or indirect effect on services." Normal changes "need to be scheduled, assessed, and authorized". Ref 5.2.4 B. Correct. A service request is "a request from a user or a user's authorized representative that initiates a service action which has been agreed as a normal part of service delivery." Ref 5.2.16 C. Incorrect. This would be supported by the 'incident management' practice. An incident is "an unplanned interruption to a service or reduction in the quality of a service." Ref 5.2.5 D. Incorrect. This would be supported by the 'problem management' practice. A problem is "a cause, or potential cause, of one or more incidents". Ref 5.2.8

135

The ITIL® 4 Foundation Examination

Q	A	Syllabus Ref	Rationale
14	D	7.1.a	A. Incorrect. The 'service level management' practice is not the responsibility of everyone in the organization. A number of roles are required but there is no fixed structure. It is recommended that there is an independent and non-aligned role where possible. Ref 5.2.15 B. Incorrect. The 'change enablement' practice is not the responsibility of everyone in the organization. Many roles can be assigned to change enablement such as change authority. It also requires input from people with specialist knowledge. Ref 5.2.4 C. Incorrect. The 'problem management' practice is not the responsibility of everyone in the organization. Most problem management activity relies on the knowledge and experience of staff. Ref 5.2.8 D. Correct. "continual improvement is everyone's responsibility" and "The commitment to and practice of continual improvement must be embedded into every fibre of the organization". Ref 5.1.2
15	D	6.1.a	A. Incorrect. "The purpose of the information security management practice is to protect the information needed by the organization to conduct its business. This includes understanding and managing risks to the confidentiality, integrity, and availability of information, as well as other aspects of information security such as authentication (ensuring someone is who they claim to be) and non-repudiation (ensuring that someone can't deny that they took an action)." Ref 5.1.3 B. Incorrect. "The purpose of the information security management practice is to protect the information needed by the organization to conduct its business. This includes understanding and managing risks to the confidentiality, integrity and availability of information, as well as other aspects of information security such as authentication (ensuring someone is who they claim to be) and non-repudiation (ensuring that someone can't deny that they took an action)." Ref 5.1.3 C. Incorrect. "The purpose of the information security management practice is to protect the information needed by the organization to conduct its business. This includes understanding and managing risks to the confidentiality, integrity and availability of information, as well as other aspects of information security such as authentication (ensuring someone is who they claim to be) and non-repudiation (ensuring that someone can't deny that they took an action)." Ref 5.1.3 D. Correct. "The purpose of the information security management practice is to protect the information needed by the organization to conduct its business. This includes understanding and managing risks to the confidentiality, integrity and availability of information, as well as other aspects of information security such as authentication (ensuring someone is who they claim to be) and non-repudiation (ensuring that someone can't deny that they took an action)." Ref 5.1.3

The ITIL® 4 Foundation Examination

Q	A	Syllabus Ref	Rationale
16	B	2.2.b	A. Incorrect. The 'focus on value' guiding principle states that "All activities conducted by the organization should link back, directly or indirectly, to value for itself, its customers, and other stakeholders." Ref 4.3.1 B. Correct. The 'start where you are' guiding principle recommends that "Services and methods already in place should be measured and/or observed directly to properly understand their current state and what can be reused from them... Getting data from the source helps to avoid assumptions which, if proven to be unfounded, can be disastrous to timelines, budgets and the quality of results." Ref 4.3.2 C. Incorrect. The 'keep it simple and practical' guiding principle states that an organization should "Always use the minimum number of steps needed to accomplish an objective." Ref 4.3.6 D. Incorrect. The 'progress iteratively with feedback principle states that "By organizing work into smaller, manageable sections that can be executed and completed in a timely manner, the focus on each effort will be sharper and easier to maintain." Ref 4.3.3
17	C	7.1.c	A. Incorrect. "There may be scripts for collecting information from users during initial contact". Ref 5.2.5 B. Incorrect. "There should be a formal process for logging and managing incidents." Ref 5.2.5 C. Correct. "This process does NOT usually include detailed procedures for how to diagnose, investigate, and resolve incidents." Ref 5.2.5 D. Incorrect. "Investigation of more complicated incidents often requires knowledge and expertise, rather than procedural steps." Ref 5.2.5
18	A	2.1	A. Correct. A guiding principle is defined as a recommendation that can guide an organization in all circumstances and will guide organizations when adopting service management. They are not described as prescriptive or mandatory. Ref 4.3 B. Incorrect. The guiding principles will be reviewed and adopted by organizations. The guiding principles guide organizations to make decisions and adopt actions. They do not mandate specific actions and decisions. Ref 4.3.8 C. Incorrect. Organizations will use the principles relevant to them and are not mandated to use a given number. Ref 4.3 D. Incorrect. The guiding principles guide organizations to make decisions and adopt actions. They are not mandatory. Ref 4.3

The ITIL® 4 Foundation Examination

Q	A	Syllabus Ref	Rationale
19	B	7.1.b	A. Incorrect. "It is essential that the correct change authority is assigned to each type of change to ensure that change enablement is both efficient and effective." For normal changes, "change models based on the type of change determine the roles for assessment and authorization". A single change authority is inadequate. Ref 5.2.4 B. Correct. "It is essential that the correct change authority is assigned to each type of change to ensure that change enablement is both efficient and effective." For normal changes, "change models based on the type of change determine the roles for assessment and authorization". Ref 5.2.4 C. Incorrect. Normal changes are "changes that need to be scheduled, assessed, and authorized following a process." Thus, all normal changes will be authorized by a change authority. Standard changes can be pre-authorized: "These are low-risk, pre-authorized changes that are well understood and fully documented, and can be implemented without needing additional authorization". Ref 5.2.4 D. Incorrect. "Emergency changes are not typically included in a change schedule, and the process for assessment and authorization is expedited to ensure they can be implemented quickly." Therefore, all emergency changes will be authorized by a change authority. Ref 5.2.4
20	C	6.1.f	A. Incorrect. "The purpose of the change enablement practice is to maximize the number of successful service and product changes by ensuring that risks have been properly assessed, authorizing changes to proceed, and managing the change schedule." Ref 5.2.4 B. Incorrect. "The purpose of the service request management practice is to support the agreed quality of a service by handling all pre-defined, user-initiated service requests in an effective and user-friendly manner". Ref 5.2.16 C. Correct. "The purpose of the release management practice is to make new and changed services and features available for use". Ref 5.2.9 D. Incorrect. "The purpose of the deployment management practice is to move new or changed hardware, software, documentation, processes, or any other component to live environments." Ref 5.3.1

The ITIL® 4 Foundation Examination

Q	A	Syllabus Ref	Rationale
21	B	5.2.a	A. Incorrect. The purpose of the 'improve' value chain activity is "to ensure continual improvement of products, services, and practices across all value chain activities and the four dimensions of service management." Ref 4.5.2 B. Correct. The purpose of the 'plan' value chain activity is "to ensure a shared understanding of the vision, current status, and improvement direction for all four dimensions and all products and services across the organization." Ref 4.5.1 C. Incorrect. The purpose of the 'deliver and support' value chain activity is "to ensure that services are delivered and supported according to agreed specifications and stakeholders' expectations." Ref 4.5.6 D. Incorrect. The purpose of the 'obtain/build' value chain activity is "to ensure that service components are available when and where they are needed, and meet agreed specifications." Ref 4.5.5
22	D	5.1	A. Incorrect. "Value chain activities use different combinations of ITIL practices". No practice belongs to a single value chain activity. Ref 4.5 B. Incorrect. Service value streams are "specific combinations of activities and practices, and each one is designed for a particular scenario" and "Service relationships include service provision, service consumption, and service relationship management." Ref 4.5, 2.4.1 C. Incorrect. Service value streams are "specific combinations of activities and practices, and each one is designed for a particular scenario." There can be multiple service value streams within one service value chain. Ref 4.5 D. Correct. "These activities represent the steps an organization takes in the creation of value. Each activity transforms inputs into outputs. These inputs can be demand from outside the value chain or outputs of other activities. All the activities are interconnected, with each activity receiving and providing triggers for further action." Ref 4.5

The ITIL® 4 Foundation Examination

Q	A	Syllabus Ref	Rationale
23	A	6.1.c	A. Correct. "The purpose of the supplier management practice is to ensure that the organization's suppliers and their performance are managed appropriately to support the seamless provision of quality products and services". Ref 5.1.13 B. Incorrect. "The purpose of the continual improvement practice is to align the organization's practices and services with changing business needs through the ongoing improvement of products, services, and practices, or any element involved in the management of products and services." This is not the purpose of the 'supplier management' practice. An organization is unlikely to change its practices to suit a supplier's needs. Ref 5.1.2 C. Incorrect. "The purpose of the relationship management practice is to establish and nurture the links between the organization and its stakeholders at strategic and tactical levels". This is not the purpose of the 'supplier management' practice. Ref 5.1.9 D. Incorrect. "The purpose of the service configuration management practice is to ensure that accurate and reliable information about the configuration of services, and the CIs that support them, is available when and where it is needed". This is not the purpose of the 'supplier management' practice. Ref 5.2.11
24	B	1.2.a	A. Incorrect. The price of the service is only part of the costs imposed on the consumer. The cost of creating the service is a concern of the service provider, not the service consumer. The service consumer should also evaluate the costs removed from the consumer. Ref 2.5.2 B. Correct. From the service consumer's perspective, there are two types of costs involved in service relationships: 1. Costs removed from the service consumer by the service (a part of the value proposition). This may include costs of staff, technology, and other resources which are not needed by the consumer. 2. Costs imposed on the consumer by the service (the costs of service consumption). The total cost of consuming a service includes the price charged by the service provider (if any), plus other costs such as staff training, costs of network utilization, procurement, etc. Ref 2.5.2 C. Incorrect. The cost of provisioning the service, and the cost of improving the service are concerns of the service provider, not the service consumer. The service consumer should evaluate the costs removed from the consumer and the costs imposed on the consumer. Ref 2.5.2 D. Incorrect. The two types of cost that a service consumer should evaluate are costs removed from the consumer and costs imposed on consumers. The cost of hardware and software may be included in either of these, but will only be part of that cost. Ref 2.5.2

The ITIL® 4 Foundation Examination

Q	A	Syllabus Ref	Rationale
25	C	6.1.n	A. Incorrect. "The purpose of the problem management practice is to reduce the likelihood and impact of incidents by identifying actual and potential causes of incidents, and managing workarounds and known errors." Ref 5.2.8 B. Incorrect. "The purpose of the change enablement practice is to maximize the number of successful service and product changes by ensuring that risks have been properly assessed, authorizing changes to proceed, and managing the change schedule." Ref 5.2.4 C. Correct. "The purpose of the service desk practice is to capture demand for incident resolution and service requests. It should also be the entry point and single point of contact for the service provider with all of its users." Ref 5.2.14 D. Incorrect. "The purpose of the service level management practice is to set clear business-based targets for service performance, so that the delivery of a service can be properly assessed, monitored, and managed against these targets." Ref 5.2.15
26	B	7.1.a	A. Incorrect. The guidance describes how there are many methods that can be used for improvement initiatives and warns against using too many. It further states that "Different types of improvement may call for different improvement methods". Therefore, using a new method each time is inappropriate. Ref 5.1.2 B. Correct. The guidance describes how there are many methods that can be used for improvement initiatives and warns against using too many. The guidance states "It is a good idea to select a few key methods that are appropriate to the types of improvement the organization typically handles and to cultivate those methods". Ref 5.1.2 C. Incorrect. The guidance describes how there are many methods that can used for improvement initiatives and warns against using too many. Ref 5.1.2 D. Incorrect. The guidance describes how there are many methods that can be used for improvement initiatives and warns against using too many. It further states that "Different types of improvements may call for different improvement methods". Therefore, selecting a single method is inappropriate. Ref 5.1.2

The ITIL® 4 Foundation Examination

Q	A	Syllabus Ref	Rationale
27	D	4.1	A. Incorrect. The seven guiding principles are 'focus on value', 'start where you are', 'progress iteratively with feedback', 'collaborate and promote visibility', 'think and work holistically', 'keep it simple and practical' and 'optimize and automate'. Ref 4.3 B. Incorrect. The four dimensions of service management are 'organizations and people', 'information and technology', 'partners and suppliers', and 'value streams and processes'. Ref 3.1-3.4 C. Incorrect. The activities of the service value chain are 'plan', 'improve', 'engage', 'design and transition', 'obtain/build', and 'deliver and support'. Ref 4.5 D. Correct. The components of the service value system are 'guiding principles', 'governance', 'service value chain', 'practices', and 'continual improvement'. Ref 4.1
28	C	7.1.f	A. Incorrect. "With increased automation, AI, robotic process automation (RPA), and chatbots, service desks are moving to provide more self-service logging and resolution directly via online portals and mobile applications." Ref 5.2.14 B. Incorrect. "The service desk may not need to be highly technical, although some are." Ref 5.2.14 C. Correct. "Another key aspect of a good service desk is its practical understanding of the wider organization, the business processes, and the users." Ref 5.2.14 D. Incorrect. "In some cases, the service desk is a tangible team, working in a single location… In other cases, a virtual service desk allows agents to work from multiple locations, geographically dispersed." Ref 5.2.14
29	C	2.2.c	A. Incorrect. The 'Focus on value' guiding principle helps to ensure that you consider all aspects of value for the service consumer, as well as the service provider and other stakeholders. It does not specifically describe organizing work into smaller, manageable sections that can be executed and completed in a timely manner. Ref 4.3.1 B. Incorrect. The 'Start where you are' guiding principle helps to avoid waste and leverage existing services, processes, people, tools, etc. It does not specifically describe organizing work into smaller, manageable sections that can be executed and completed in a timely manner. Ref 4.3.2 C. Correct. The description of the 'progress iteratively with feedback' guiding principle says "by organizing work into smaller, manageable sections that can be executed and completed in a timely manner, the focus on each effort will be sharper and easier to maintain." Ref 4.3.3 D. Incorrect. The 'collaborate and promote visibility' guiding principle helps to involve the right people and provide better decision-making and greater likelihood of success. It does not specifically describe organizing work into smaller, manageable sections that can be executed and completed in a timely manner. Ref 4.3.4

The ITIL® 4 Foundation Examination

Q	A	Syllabus Ref	Rationale
30	A	7.1.b	A. Correct. "These are low-risk, pre-authorized changes that are well understood and fully documented, and can be implemented without needing additional authorization. They are often initiated as service requests, but may also be operational changes. When the procedure for a standard change is created or modified, there should be a full risk assessment and authorization as for any other change. This risk assessment does not need to be repeated each time the standard change is implemented; it only needs to be done if there is a modification to the way it is carried out." Ref 5.2.4 B. Incorrect. Normal changes are "changes that need to be scheduled, assessed, and authorized." Ref 5.2.4 C. Incorrect. An emergency change that is needed to resolve an incident should still be assessed and authorized. "As far as possible, emergency changes should be subject to the same testing, assessment, and authorization as normal changes". Ref 5.2.4 D. Incorrect. This is a description of a normal change: "changes that need to be scheduled, assessed, and authorized". Ref 5.2.4
31	C	7.1.d	A. Incorrect. A change request is only raised if it is justified. "Error control also includes identification of potential permanent solutions which may result in a change request for implementation of a solution, but only if this can be justified in terms of cost, risks, and benefits". Ref 5.2.8 B. Incorrect. The 'incident management' practice restores service not the 'problem management' practice. "The purpose of the incident management practice is to minimize the negative impact of incidents by restoring normal service operation as quickly as possible.". Ref 5.2.5 C. Correct. "An effective incident workaround can become a permanent way of dealing with some problems when resolving the problem is not viable or cost-effective. In this case, the problem remains in the known error status, and the documented workaround is applied should related incidents occur". Ref 5.2.8 D. Incorrect. The problem record is not deleted. "Workarounds are documented in problem records". ".. the problem remains in the known error status, and the documented workaround is applied should related incidents occur". Ref 5.2.8

The ITIL® 4 Foundation Examination

Q	A	Syllabus Ref	Rationale
32	A	6.2.d	A. Correct. A change is the "addition, modification, or removal of anything that could have a direct or indirect effect on services". Ref 5.2.4 B. Incorrect. "The purpose of the service configuration management practice is to ensure that accurate and reliable information about the configuration of services, and the CIs that support them, is available when and where it is needed." Ref 5.2.11 C. Incorrect. "The purpose of the release management practice is to make new and changed services and features available for use". Ref 5.2.9 D. Incorrect. "The purpose of the deployment management practice is to move new or changed hardware, software, documentation, processes, or any other component to live environments." Ref 5.3.1
33	A	6.2.b	A. Correct. "An event can be defined as any change of state that has significance for the management of a service or other configuration item (CI)". Ref 5.2.7 B. Incorrect. The definition of a configuration item is "any component that needs to be managed in order to deliver an IT service." Ref 5.2.11 C. Incorrect. An incident is "An unplanned interruption to a service or reduction in the quality of a service." Ref 5.2.5 D. Incorrect. An IT asset is "Any financially valuable component that can contribute to the delivery of an IT product or service." Ref 5.2.11
34	C	1.2.d	A. Incorrect. "A tangible or intangible deliverable of an activity" is the definition of an output, not an outcome. Ref 2.5.1 B. Incorrect. "The functionality offered by a product or service to meet a particular need" is the definition of utility, not an outcome. The utility of the service may facilitate outcomes. Ref 2.5.4 C. Correct. An outcome is "a result for a stakeholder enabled by one or more outputs". The definition of a service describes how the value of a service enables value co-creation by facilitating outcomes that customers want to achieve. Ref 2.5.1 D. Incorrect. A product is "a configuration of an organization's resources designed to offer value for a consumer." Ref 2.3.1

The ITIL® 4 Foundation Examination

Q	A	Syllabus Ref	Rationale
35	D	3.1.b	A. Incorrect. "The challenges of information management, such as those presented by security and regulatory compliance requirements, are also a focus of [the 'information and technology] dimension". Ref 3.2 B. Incorrect. "The technologies that support service management include, but are not limited to, workflow management systems, knowledge bases, inventory systems, communication systems, and analytical tools". Ref 3.2 C. Incorrect. "The technologies that support service management include, but are not limited to, workflow management systems, knowledge bases, inventory systems, communication systems, and analytical tools." Ref 3.2 D. Correct. "The organizations and people dimension of a service covers roles and responsibilities, formal organizational structures, culture, and required staffing and competencies, all of which are related to the creation, delivery, and improvement of a service." Ref 3.1
36	D	7.1.d	D. Correct. (1) "Problem management activities can identify improvement opportunities in all four dimensions of service management. Solutions can in some cases be treated as improvement opportunities, so they are included in a continual improvement register (CIR), and continual improvement techniques are used to prioritize and manage them." (4) "Error control also includes identification of potential permanent solutions which may result in a change request for implementation of a solution." Ref 5.2.8 A, B C. Incorrect. (2) "The purpose of the service request management practice is to support the agreed quality of a service by handling all pre-defined, user-initiated service requests in an effective and user-friendly manner." Ref 5.2.16 (3) "The purpose of the service level management practice is to set clear business-based targets for service levels, and to ensure that delivery of services is properly assessed, monitored, and managed against these targets." Ref 5.2.15

The ITIL® 4 Foundation Examination

Q	A	Syllabus Ref	Rationale
37	B	2.2.f	A. Incorrect. "Trying to provide a solution for every exception will often lead to over-complication. When creating a process or a service, designers need to think about exceptions, but they cannot cover them all. Instead, rules should be designed that can be used to handle exceptions generally." Ref 4.3.6 B. Correct. The 'keep it simple and practical' guiding principle states: "When analyzing a practice, process, service, metric, or other improvement target, always ask whether it contributes to value creation." Ref 4.3.6.1 C. Incorrect. "When designing, managing, or operating practices, be mindful of conflicting objectives ... the organization should agree on a balance between its competing objectives." Ref 4.3.6.2 D. Incorrect. "It is better to start with an uncomplicated approach and then carefully add controls, activities, or metrics when it is seen that they are truly needed." Ref 4.3.6.1
38	C	2.2.a	A. Incorrect. It is essential to determine who the service consumer is, and what they value. The outcomes should be based on this understanding, rather than determining them. "The first step in focusing on value is knowing who is being served. In each situation the service provider must, therefore, determine who the service consumer is". Ref 4.3.1.1 B. Incorrect. Suppliers and partners are possible stakeholders, but it is important to identify the service consumer first. "The first step in focusing on value is knowing who is being served. In each situation the service provider must, therefore, determine who the service consumer is". Ref 4.3.1.1 C. Correct. "The first step in focusing on value is knowing who is being served. In each situation the service provider must, therefore, determine who the service consumer is". Ref 4.3.1.1 D. Incorrect. The cost of providing the service may have some impact on the value from the perspective of the service provider. But "The first step in focusing on value is knowing who is being served. In each situation the service provider must, therefore, determine who the service consumer is". Ref 4.3.1.1

The ITIL® 4 Foundation Examination

Q	A	Syllabus Ref	Rationale
39	D	1.3.a	A. Incorrect. The combination of things described in this option may help to create value, but it is not an example of value. Value is "the perceived benefits, usefulness and importance of something." Ref 2.1 B. Incorrect. The combination of things described in this option may help to create an outcome, but it is not an example of an outcome. Outcome is "a result for a stakeholder enabled by one or more outputs." Ref 2.5.1 C. Incorrect. Warranty is "assurance that a product or service will meet agreed requirements." New functionality may or may not affect warranty. Ref 2.5.4 D. Correct. Service providers define combinations of goods, access to resources and service actions, to address the needs of different consumer groups. These combinations are called service offerings. Ref 2.3.2
40	B	1.1.c	A. Incorrect. An output is "A tangible or intangible deliverable of an activity". Ref 2.5.1 B. Correct. Warranty is "assurance that a product or service will meet agreed requirements." Ref 2.5.4 C. Incorrect. A risk is "a possible event that could cause harm or loss, or make it more difficult to achieve objectives". Ref 2.5.3 D. Incorrect. Utility is "the functionality offered by a product or service to meet a particular need". Ref 2.5.4

The ITIL® 4 Foundation Examination

Sample Paper 2

Question Booklet

Multiple Choice

Examination Duration: 1 hour

Instructions

1. You should attempt all 40 questions. Each question is worth one mark.
2. There is only one correct answer per question.
3. You need to answer 26 questions correctly to pass the exam.
4. Mark your answers on the answer sheet provided. Use a pencil (NOT pen).
5. You have 1 hour to complete this exam.
6. This is a 'closed book' exam. No material other than the exam paper is allowed.

The ITIL® 4 Foundation Examination

1) What is the effect of increased automation on the 'service desk' practice?

   A. Greater ability to focus on customer experience when personal contact is needed
   B. Decrease in self-service incident logging and resolution
   C. Increased ability to focus on fixing technology instead of supporting people
   D. Elimination of the need to escalate incidents to support teams

2) Which term describes the functionality offered by a service?

   A. Cost
   B. Utility
   C. Warranty
   D. Risk

3) Which is the purpose of the 'monitoring and event management' practice?

   A. To ensure that accurate and reliable information about the configuration of services is available when and where it is needed
   B. To systematically observe services and service components, and record and report selected changes of state
   C. To protect the information needed by the organization to conduct its business
   D. To minimize the negative impact of incidents by restoring normal service operation as quickly as possible

4) What should all 'continual improvement' decisions be based on?

   A. Details of how services are measured
   B. Accurate and carefully analyzed data
   C. An up-to-date balanced scorecard
   D. A recent maturity assessment

5) How do all value chain activities transform inputs to outputs?

   A. By determining service demand
   B. By using a combination of practices
   C. By using a single functional team
   D. By implementing process automation

6) How does customer engagement contribute to the 'service level management' practice?

   1. It captures information that metrics can be based on
   2. It ensures the organization meets defined service levels
   3. It defines the workflows for service requests
   4. It supports progress discussions

   A. 1 and 2
   B. 2 and 3
   C. 3 and 4
   D. 1 and 4

7) What is the starting point for optimization?

   A. Securing stakeholder engagement
   B. Understanding the vision and objectives of the organization
   C. Determining where the most positive impact would be
   D. Standardizing practices and services

8) Identify the missing words in the following sentence.

   The purpose of the [?] is to ensure that the organization continually co-creates value with all stakeholders in line with the organization's objectives.

   A. 'focus on value' guiding principle
   B. four dimensions of service management
   C. service value system
   D. 'service request management' practice

9) Which practice provides support for managing feedback, compliments and complaints from users?

   A. Change enablement
   B. Service request management
   C. Problem management
   D. Incident management

10) Which joint activity performed by a service provider and service consumer ensures continual value co-creation?

    A. Service provision
    B. Service consumption
    C. Service offering
    D. Service relationship management

11) Which practice may involve the initiation of disaster recovery?

    A. Incident management
    B. Service request management
    C. Service level management
    D. IT asset management

12) What type of change is MOST likely to be managed by the 'service request management' practice?

    A. A normal change
    B. An emergency change
    C. A standard change
    D. An application change

13) Which guiding principle emphasizes the need to understand the flow of work in progress, identify bottlenecks, and uncover waste?

   A. Focus on value
   B. Collaborate and promote visibility
   C. Think and work holistically
   D. Keep it simple and practical

14) What is a means of enabling value co-creation by facilitating outcomes that customers want to achieve?

   A. A service
   B. An output
   C. A practice
   D. Continual improvement

15) Which statement about change authorization is CORRECT?

   A. A change authority should be assigned to each type of change and change model
   B. Centralizing change authorization to a single person is the most effective means of authorization
   C. The authorization of normal changes should be expedited to ensure they can be implemented quickly
   D. Standard changes are high risk and should be authorized by the highest level of change authority

16) Which dimension of service management considers governance, management, and communication?

   A. Organizations and people
   B. Information and technology
   C. Partners and suppliers
   D. Value streams and processes

17) Identify the missing word in the following sentence.

A known error is a problem that has been [?] and has not been resolved.

A. logged
B. analyzed
C. escalated
D. closed

18) Which statement about known errors and problems is CORRECT?

A. Known error is the status assigned to a problem after it has been analyzed
B. A known error is the cause of one or more problems
C. Known errors cause vulnerabilities, problems cause incidents
D. Known errors are managed by technical staff, problems are managed by service management staff

19) What does the 'service request management' practice depend on for maximum efficiency?

A. Compliments and complaints
B. Self-service tools
C. Processes and procedures
D. Incident management

20) Which statement about the 'service desk' practice is CORRECT?

A. It provides a link with stakeholders at strategic and tactical levels
B. It carries out change assessment and authorization
C. It investigates the cause of incidents
D. It needs a practical understanding of the business processes

21) Which practice ensures that accurate and reliable information is available about configuration items and the relationships between them?

   A. Service configuration management
   B. Service desk
   C. IT asset management
   D. Monitoring and event management

22) Which practice has a purpose that includes restoring normal service operation as quickly as possible?

   A. Supplier management
   B. Deployment management
   C. Problem management
   D. Incident management

23) Identify the missing word in the following sentence.

   A customer is the role that defines the requirements for a service and takes responsibility for the [?] of service consumption.

   A. outputs
   B. outcomes
   C. costs
   D. risks

24) Which guiding principle describes the importance of doing something, instead of spending a long time analyzing different options?

   A. Optimize and automate
   B. Start where you are
   C. Focus on value
   D. Progress iteratively with feedback

25) What should be done for every problem?

   A. It should be diagnosed to identify possible solutions
   B. It should be prioritized based on its potential impact and probability
   C. It should be resolved so that it can be closed
   D. It should have a workaround to reduce the impact

26) How should an organization include third-party suppliers in the continual improvement of services?

   A. Ensure suppliers include details of their approach to service improvement in contracts
   B. Require evidence that the supplier uses agile development methods
   C. Require evidence that the supplier implements all improvements using project management practices
   D. Ensure that all supplier problem management activities result in improvements

27) What considerations influence the supplier strategy of an organization?

   A. Contracts and agreements
   B. Type of cooperation with suppliers
   C. Corporate culture of the organization
   D. Level of formality

28) What is a problem?

   A. An addition or modification that could have an effect on services
   B. Any change of state that has significance for the management of a configuration item
   C. A cause or potential cause of one or more incidents
   D. An unplanned reduction in the quality of a service

29) What is the purpose of the 'relationship management' practice?

    A. To align the organization's practices and services with changing business needs
    B. To establish and nurture the links between the organization and its stakeholders at strategic and tactical levels
    C. To reduce the likelihood and impact of incidents by identifying actual and potential causes of incidents, and managing workarounds and known errors
    D. To minimize the negative impact of incidents by restoring normal service operation as quickly as possible

30) Which is intended to help an organization adopt and adapt ITIL guidance?

    A. The four dimensions of service management
    B. The guiding principles
    C. The service value chain
    D. Practices

31) What is an output?

    A. A change of state that has significance for the management of a configuration item
    B. A possible event that could cause harm or loss
    C. A result for a stakeholder
    D. Something created by carrying out an activity

32) What is the reason for using a balanced bundle of service metrics?

    A. It reduces the number of metrics that need to be collected
    B. It reports each service element separately
    C. It provides an outcome-based view of services
    D. It facilitates the automatic collection of metrics

33) Why should incidents be prioritized?

   A. To help automated matching of incidents to problems or known errors
   B. To identify which support team the incident should be escalated to
   C. To ensure that incidents with the highest business impact are resolved first
   D. To encourage a high level of collaboration within and between teams

34) Which practice has a purpose that includes helping the organization to maximize value, control costs and manage risks?

   A. Relationship management
   B. IT asset management
   C. Release management
   D. Service desk

35) Why should service desk staff detect recurring issues?

   A. To help identify problems
   B. To escalate incidents to the correct support team
   C. To ensure effective handling of service requests
   D. To engage the correct change authority

36) Which value chain activity communicates the current status of all four dimensions of service management?

   A. Improve
   B. Engage
   C. Obtain/build
   D. Plan

37) Which guiding principle is PRIMARILY concerned with consumer's revenue and growth?

   A. Keep it simple and practical
   B. Optimize and automate
   C. Progress iteratively with feedback
   D. Focus on value

38) Which practice provides visibility of the organization's services by capturing and reporting on service performance?

   A. Service desk
   B. Service level management
   C. Service request management
   D. Service configuration management

39) Which is the BEST example of an emergency change?

   A. The implementation of a planned new release of a software application
   B. A low-risk computer upgrade implemented as a service request
   C. The implementation of a security patch to a critical software application
   D. A scheduled major hardware and software implementation

40) Which guiding principle recommends assessing the current state and deciding what can be reused?

   A. Focus on value
   B. Start where you are
   C. Collaborate and promote visibility
   D. Progress iteratively with feedback

The ITIL® 4 Foundation Examination

Sample Paper 2

Answers and Rationales

The ITIL® 4 Foundation Examination

For exam paper: EN_ITIL4_FND_2019_SamplePaper2_QuestionBk_v1.2

Q	A	Syllabus Ref	Rationale
1	A	7.1.f	A. Correct. "With increased automation... The impact on service desks is reduced phone contact, less low-level work, and a greater ability to focus on excellent CX when personal contact is needed". Ref 5.2.14 B. Incorrect. The effect of automation is to increase self-service, not to decrease it. "With increased automation, AI, robotic process automation (RPA), and chatbots, service desks are moving to provide more self-service logging and resolution directly via online portals and mobile applications". Ref 5.2.14 C. Incorrect. The opposite is true. "With increased automation and the gradual removal of technical debt, the focus of the service desk is to provide support for 'people and business' rather than simply technical issues". Ref 5.2.14 D. Incorrect. The use of automation will not eliminate the need to escalate incidents. "A key point to be understood is that, no matter how efficient the service desk and its people are, there will always be issues that need escalation and underpinning support from other teams". Ref 5.2.14
2	B	1.2.g	A. Incorrect. Cost is "The amount of money spent on a specific activity or resource." Ref 2.5.2 B. Correct. Utility is "The functionality offered by a product or service." Ref 2.5.4 C. Incorrect. Warranty is "Assurance that a product or service will meet agreed requirements". Ref 2.5.4 D. Incorrect. A risk is "A possible event that could cause harm or loss, or make it more difficult to achieve objectives". Ref 2.5.3
3	B	6.1.e	A. Incorrect. "The purpose of the service configuration management practice is to ensure that accurate and reliable information about the configuration of services, and the CIs that support them, is available when and where it is needed". Ref 5.2.11 B. Correct. "The purpose of the monitoring and event management practice is to systematically observe services and service components, and record and report selected changes of state identified as events". Ref 5.2.7 C. Incorrect. "The purpose of the information security management practice is to protect the information needed by the organization to conduct its business". Ref 5.1.3 D. Incorrect. "The purpose of the incident management practice is to minimize the negative impact of incidents by restoring normal service operation as quickly as possible". Ref 5.2.5

The ITIL® 4 Foundation Examination

Q	A	Syllabus Ref	Rationale
4	B	7.1.a	A. Incorrect. How services are measured is important, however only accurate data can drive fact-based decisions for improvement. Ref 5.1.2 B. Correct. "Accurate data, carefully analyzed and understood, is the foundation of fact-based decision-making for improvement." The 'continual improvement' practice should be supported by relevant data sources and by skilled data analytics to ensure that each potential improvement situation is sufficiently understood. Ref 5.1.2 C. Incorrect. A balanced scorecard is one input to making a decision, but on its own it does not serve as the foundation for fact-based decisions. Ref 5.1.2 D. Incorrect. Maturity assessments are useful but they provide only one piece of information, as opposed to providing the foundations for decision-making in the continual improvement practice. Ref 5.1.2
5	B	5.1	A. Incorrect. Demand is the input to the service value chain. Value chain activities "represent the steps an organization takes in the creation of value. Each activity contributes to the value chain by transforming specific inputs into outputs." Ref 4.5 B. Correct. "To convert inputs into outputs, the value chain activities use different combinations of ITIL practices." Ref 4.5 C. Incorrect. It uses various resources from different practices when needed. "To convert inputs into outputs, the value chain activities use different combinations of ITIL practices (sets of resources for performing certain types of work), drawing on internal or third-party resources, processes, skills, and competencies as required." Ref 4.5 D. Incorrect. The 'optimize and automate' guiding principle recommends that activities should be automated where this is practical but the service value chain does not require automation. "Technology should not always be relied upon without the capability of human intervention, as automation for automation's sake can increase costs and reduce organizational robustness and resilience." Ref 4.3.7

The ITIL® 4 Foundation Examination

Q	A	Syllabus Ref	Rationale
6	D	7.1.g	D. Correct. (1) (4) "Customer engagement: This involves initial listening, discovery, and information capture on which to base metrics, measurement, and ongoing progress discussions." Ref 5.2.15 A, B, C. Incorrect. (2) Service level management "ensures the organization meets the defined service levels through the collection, analysis, storage, and reporting of the relevant metrics for the identified services," not just through customer engagement. Ref 5.2.15 (3) It may define the requirements for service requests but defining the workflow is part of 'service request management'. "When new service requests need to be added to the service catalogue, existing workflow models should be leveraged whenever possible." Ref 5.2.16
7	B	2.2.g	A. Incorrect. This is step 4 of the principle 'optimize and automate': "Ensure the optimization has the appropriate level of stakeholder engagement and commitment." Ref 4.3.7.1 B. Correct. The first step of the principle 'optimize and automate' is: "Understand and agree the context in which the proposed optimization exists. This includes agreeing the overall vision and objectives of the organization." Ref 4.3.7.1 C. Incorrect. This is step 2 of the principle 'optimize and automate': "Assess the current state of the proposed optimization. This will help to understand where it can be improved and which improvement opportunities are likely to produce the biggest positive impact." Ref 4.3.7.1 D. Incorrect. This is step 3 of the principle 'optimize and automate': "Agree what the future state and priorities of the organization should be, focusing on simplification and value. This typically also includes standardization of practices and services, which will make it easier to automate or optimize further at a later point." Ref 4.3.7.1

The ITIL® 4 Foundation Examination

Q	A	Syllabus Ref	Rationale
8	C	4.1	A. Incorrect. The 'focus on value' guiding principle guides an organization to consider the needs of the service consumer. It cannot ensure that the organization continually co-creates value with all stakeholders. Ref 4.3.1 B. Incorrect. The four dimensions "represent perspectives which are relevant to the whole SVS, including the entirety of the service value chain and all ITIL practices." They do not ensure that the organization continually co-creates value with all stakeholders. Ref 3 C. Correct. "The purpose of the SVS is to ensure that the organization continually co-creates value with all stakeholders through the use and management of products and services." Ref 4.1 D. Incorrect. The purpose of the 'service request management' practice is to "support the agreed quality of a service by handling all pre-defined, user-initiated service requests in an effective and user-friendly manner." It doesn't ensure that the organization continually co-creates value with all stakeholders. Ref 5.2.16
9	B	7.1.e	A. Incorrect. "The purpose of the change enablement practice is to maximize the number of successful service and product changes by ensuring that risks have been properly assessed, authorizing changes to proceed, and managing the change schedule." Ref 5.2.4 B. Correct. "The purpose of the service request management practice is to support the agreed quality of a service by handling all pre-defined, user-initiated service requests in an effective and user-friendly manner," and "Each service request may include one or more of the following: ... feedback, compliments, and complaints (for example, complaints about a new interface or compliments to a support team)." Ref 5.2.16 C. Incorrect. "The purpose of the problem management practice is to reduce the likelihood and impact of incidents by identifying actual and potential causes of incidents, and managing workarounds and known errors." Ref 5.2.8 D. Incorrect. "The purpose of the incident management practice is to minimize the negative impact of incidents by restoring normal service operation as quickly as possible." Ref 5.2.5

The ITIL® 4 Foundation Examination

Q	A	Syllabus Ref	Rationale
10	D	1.3.b	A. Incorrect. Service provision is not a joint activity; it is performed by a service provider. Ref 2.4.1 B. Incorrect. Service consumption is not a joint activity; it is performed by a service consumer. Ref 2.4.1 C. Incorrect. Service offering is not an activity; it is "A description of one or more services, designed to address the needs of a target consumer group. A service offering may include goods, access to resources, and service actions". Ref 2.3.2 D. Correct. Service relationship management is "Joint activities performed by a service provider and a service consumer to ensure continual value co-creation based on agreed and available service offerings". Ref 2.4.1
11	A	7.1.c	A. Correct. "In some extreme cases, disaster recovery plans may be invoked to resolve an incident." Ref 5.2.5 B. Incorrect. "Service requests are a normal part of service delivery and are not a failure or degradation of service, which are handled as incidents." Ref 5.2.16 C. Incorrect. "The purpose of the service level management practice is to set clear business-based targets for service levels, and to ensure that delivery of services is properly assessed, monitored, and managed against these targets." Ref 5.2.15 D. Incorrect. "The purpose of the IT asset management practice is to plan and manage the full lifecycle of all IT assets." Asset management "includes the acquisition, operation, care and disposal of organizational assets." Ref 5.2.6
12	C	7.1.e	A. Incorrect. "Normal changes: These are changes that need to be scheduled, assessed, and authorized". This is supported by the 'change enablement' practice, not by 'service request management'. Ref 5.2.4 B. Incorrect. "As far as possible, emergency changes should be subject to the same testing, assessment, and authorization as normal changes." This is supported by the 'change enablement' practice, not by 'service request management'. Ref 5.2.4 C. Correct. "Fulfilment of service requests may include changes to services or their components; usually these are standard changes." and "Standard changes: These are low-risk, pre-authorized changes that are well understood and fully documented, and can be implemented without needing additional authorization. They are often initiated as service requests". Ref 5.2.16, 5.2.4 D. Incorrect. "The scope of change enablement is defined by each organization. It will typically include all IT infrastructure, applications, documentation, processes". Some application changes may be managed as standard changes, but others will be normal or emergency changes and will be supported by the 'change enablement' practice. Ref 5.2.4

164

The ITIL® 4 Foundation Examination

Q	A	Syllabus Ref	Rationale
13	B	2.2.d	A. Incorrect. 'Focus on value' states that all improvement work should deliver measurable value for customers and other stakeholders, but it does not specifically highlight the need to understand the flow of work, identify bottlenecks, and uncover waste. Ref 4.3.1 B. Correct. 'Collaborate and promote' visibility states "Insufficient visibility of work leads to poor decision-making, which in turn impacts the organization's ability to improve internal capabilities. It will then become difficult to drive improvements as it will not be clear which ones are likely to have the greatest positive impact on results. To avoid this, the organization needs to perform such critical analysis activities as: understanding the flow of work in progress; identifying bottlenecks, as well as excess capacity; and uncovering waste". Ref 4.3.4.3 C. Incorrect. 'Think and work holistically' states that the organization should work in an integrated way on the whole, not just on the parts, but it does not specifically highlight the need to understand the flow of work, identify bottlenecks, and uncover waste. Ref 4.3.5 D. Incorrect. 'Keep it simple and practical' states that the organization should use the minimum number of steps, and eliminate steps that produce no useful outcome. This does imply that you should uncover waste, but it does not specifically highlight the need to understand the flow of work and identify bottlenecks. Ref 4.3.6
14	A	1.1.a	A. Correct. A service is "A means of enabling value co-creation by facilitating outcomes that customers want to achieve, without the customer having to manage specific costs and risks." Ref 2.3.1 B. Incorrect. An output is "A tangible or intangible deliverable of an activity." Ref 2.5.1 C. Incorrect. Practices are "Sets of organizational resources designed for performing work or accomplishing an objective." Ref 4.1 D. Incorrect. 'Continual improvement' is a practice "to align the organization's practices and services with changing business needs." Ref 5.1.2

The ITIL® 4 Foundation Examination

Q	A	Syllabus Ref	Rationale
15	A	7.1.b	A. Correct. "It is essential that the correct change authority is assigned to each type of change to ensure that change enablement is both efficient and effective." Ref 5.2.4 B. Incorrect. There is no rule that centralizing change authority is the most effective method. In some cases, decentralizing decision-making is better: "In high-velocity organizations, it is a common practice to decentralize change approval, making the peer review a top predictor of high performance." Ref 5.2.4 C. Incorrect. This answer confuses normal changes with emergency changes. "Emergency changes are not typically included in a change schedule, and the process for assessment and authorization is expedited to ensure they can be implemented quickly." Ref 5.2.4 D. Incorrect. Standard changes are usually low risk and pre-authorized. "These are low-risk, pre-authorized changes that are well understood and fully documented, and can be implemented without needing additional authorization." Ref 5.2.4
16	A	3.1.a	A. Correct. "It is important to ensure that the way an organization is structured and managed, as well as its roles, responsibilities, and systems of authority and communication, is well defined and supports its overall strategy and operating model." Ref 3.1 B. Incorrect. The 'information and technology' dimension "includes the information and knowledge necessary for the management of services, as well as the technologies required. It also incorporates the relationships between different components of the SVS, such as the inputs and outputs of activities and practices." Ref 3.2 C. Incorrect. "The partners and suppliers dimension encompasses an organization's relationships with other organizations that are involved in the design, development, deployment, delivery, support and/or continual improvement of services. It also incorporates contracts and other agreements between the organization and its partners or suppliers." Ref 3.3 D. Incorrect. The 'value streams and processes' dimension "is concerned with how the various parts of the organization work in an integrated and coordinated way to enable value creation through products and services." Ref 3.4

The ITIL® 4 Foundation Examination

Q	A	Syllabus Ref	Rationale
17	B	6.2.g	A. Incorrect. A known error is "A problem that has been analyzed but has not been resolved". If a problem has been logged but not analyzed, it would not be considered a known error. Ref 5.2.8 B. Correct. A known error is "A problem that has been analyzed but has not been resolved". Ref 5.2.8 C. Incorrect. A known error is "A problem that has been analyzed but has not been resolved" – it may or may not be escalated. Ref 5.2.8 D. Incorrect. A known error is "A problem that has been analyzed but has not been resolved". If a problem has been closed, it would not be considered a known error. Ref 5.2.8
18	A	7.1.d	A. Correct. Known errors "are problems where initial analysis has been completed; it usually means that faulty components have been identified… the problem remains in the known error status, and the documented workaround is applied". Ref 5.2.8 B. Incorrect. A problem is "A cause, or potential cause, of one or more incidents." A known error is "A problem that has been analyzed but has not been resolved." Known errors do not cause problems; they are problems that have been analyzed but not yet resolved. Ref 5.2.8 C. Incorrect. Both known errors and problems cause incidents. A problem is "A cause, or potential cause, of one or more incidents." A known error is "A problem that has been analyzed but has not been resolved." Both problems and known errors may be vulnerabilities: "Every service has errors, flaws, or vulnerabilities that may cause incidents." Ref 5.2.8 D. Incorrect. "Many problem management activities rely on the knowledge and experience of staff, rather than on following detailed procedures. People responsible for diagnosing problems often need the ability to understand complex systems, and to think about how different failures might have occurred. Developing this combination of analytic and creative ability requires mentoring and time, as well as suitable training." These people might work in a technical role, or in a service management role. Ref 5.2.8
19	C	7.1.e	A. Incorrect. Compliments and complaints are examples of service requests. The efficiency of the practice does not depend on them. Ref 5.2.16 B. Incorrect. Many service requests are initiated and fulfilled using self-service tools, but not all are appropriate for this approach. Ref 5.2.16 C. Correct. "Service request management is dependent upon well-designed processes and procedures, which are operationalized through tracking and automation tools to maximize the efficiency of the practice." Ref 5.2.16 D. Incorrect. "Service requests are a normal part of service delivery and are not a failure or degradation of service, which are handled as incidents." Ref 5.2.16

The ITIL® 4 Foundation Examination

Q	A	Syllabus Ref	Rationale
20	D	7.1.f	A. Incorrect. This is a purpose of 'relationship management': "to establish and nurture the links between the organization and its stakeholders at strategic and tactical levels." Ref 5.1.9 B. Incorrect. "Service desks provide a clear path for users to report issues, queries, and requests, and have them acknowledged, classified, owned, and actioned." This does not include the assessment and authorization of changes. This will be provided by the 'change enablement' practice. Ref 5.2.14 C. Incorrect. Investigating the cause of incidents is a purpose of 'problem management'. "The purpose of the problem management practice is to reduce the likelihood and impact of incidents by identifying actual and potential causes of incidents." Ref 5.2.8 D. Correct. "Another key aspect of a good service desk is its practical understanding of the wider organization, the business processes, and the users." Ref 5.2.14
21	A	6.1.g	A. Correct. "The purpose of the service configuration management practice is to ensure that accurate and reliable information about the configuration of services, and the CIs that support them, is available when and where it is needed. This includes information on how CIs are configured and the relationships between them". Ref 5.2.11 B. Incorrect. "The purpose of the service desk practice is to capture demand for incident resolution and service requests". Ref 5.2.14 C. Incorrect. "The purpose of the IT asset management practice is to plan and manage the full lifecycle of all IT assets, to help the organization: maximize value, control costs, manage risks, support decision-making about purchase, re-use, and disposal of assets". Ref 5.2.6 D. Incorrect. "The purpose of the monitoring and event management practice is to systematically observe services and service components, and record and report selected changes of state identified as events". Ref 5.2.7

The ITIL® 4 Foundation Examination

Q	A	Syllabus Ref	Rationale
22	D	6.1.k	A. Incorrect. "The purpose of the supplier management practice is to ensure that the organization's suppliers and their performances are managed appropriately to support the seamless provision of quality products and services." Ref 5.1.13 B. Incorrect. "The purpose of the deployment management practice is to move new or changed hardware, software, documentation, processes, or any other component to live environments. It may also be involved in deploying components to other environments, for testing or staging." Ref 5.3.1 C. Incorrect. "The purpose of the problem management practice is to reduce the likelihood and impact of incidents by identifying actual and potential causes of incidents, and managing workarounds and known errors." Ref 5.2.8 D. Correct. "The purpose of the incident management practice is to minimize the negative impact of incidents by restoring normal service operation as quickly as possible." Ref 5.2.5
23	B	1.1.d	A. Incorrect. "Customer: The role that defines the requirements for a service and takes responsibility for the outcomes of service consumption." Ref 2.2.2 B. Correct. "Customer: The role that defines the requirements for a service and takes responsibility for the outcomes of service consumption." Ref 2.2.2 C. Incorrect. "Customer: The role that defines the requirements for a service and takes responsibility for the outcomes of service consumption." Ref 2.2.2 D. Incorrect. "Customer: The role that defines the requirements for a service and takes responsibility for the outcomes of service consumption." Ref 2.2.2
24	D	2.2.c	A. Incorrect. 'Optimize and automate' says that you should understand and optimize something before you automate it. "Attempting to automate something that is complex or suboptimal is unlikely to achieve the desired outcome." Ref 4.3.7.3 B. Incorrect. 'Start where you are' says that you should understand the current situation before making changes. "Services and methods already in place should be measured and/or observed directly to properly understand their current state and what can be re-used from them. Decisions on how to proceed should be based on information that is as accurate as possible." Ref 4.3.2.1 C. Incorrect. 'Focus on value' says that each improvement iteration should create value for stakeholders "All activities conducted by the organization should link back, directly or indirectly, to value for itself, its customers, and other stakeholders." Ref 4.3.1 D. Correct. 'Progress iteratively with feedback' recommends comprehending "the whole, but do something: Sometimes the greatest enemy to progressing iteratively is the desire to understand and account for everything. This can lead to what has sometimes been called 'analysis paralysis', in which so much time is spent analyzing the situation that nothing ever gets done about it." Ref 4.3.3.3

The ITIL® 4 Foundation Examination

Q	A	Syllabus Ref	Rationale
25	B	7.1.d	A. Incorrect. "It is not essential to analyze every problem; it is more valuable to make significant progress on the highest-priority problems than to investigate every minor problem that the organization is aware of." Ref 5.2.8 B. Correct. "Problems are prioritized for analysis based on the risk that they pose, and are managed as risks based on their potential impact and probability." Ref 5.2.8 C. Incorrect. "Error control also includes identification of potential permanent solutions which may result in a change request for implementation of a solution, but only if this can be justified in terms of cost, risks, and benefits." Ref 5.2.8 D. Incorrect. "When a problem cannot be resolved quickly, it is often useful to find and document a workaround for future incidents, based on an understanding of the problem." Ref 5.2.8
26	A	7.1.a	A. Correct "When contracting for a supplier's service, the contract should include details of how they will measure, report on, and improve their services over the life of the contract." Ref 5.1.2 B. Incorrect. Agile methods do take an incremental approach, as they "focus on making improvements incrementally at a cadence"; however, this alone would not guarantee a supplier is committed to continual improvement. Ref 5.1.2 C. Incorrect. Many improvement initiatives use project management practices, but it may not be practical to do so for some. "Many improvement initiatives will use project management practices to organize and manage their execution", but not all improvement initiatives. Ref 5.1.2 D. Incorrect. Many 'problem management' activities will result in improvements, however not all supplier problems will result in improvements, so this is not a sensible approach. "It is not essential to analyze every problem; it is more valuable to make significant progress on the highest-priority problems than to investigate every minor problem that the organization is aware of." Ref 5.2.8

The ITIL® 4 Foundation Examination

Q	A	Syllabus Ref	Rationale
27	C	3.1.c	A. Incorrect. "The partners and suppliers dimension encompasses an organization's relationships with other organizations that are involved in the design, development, deployment, delivery, support and/or continual improvement of services. It also incorporates contracts and other agreements between the organization and its partners or suppliers." These considerations depend on the supplier strategy, rather than influence it. Ref 3.3 B. Incorrect. The type of cooperation with suppliers depends on the supplier strategy, rather than influence it. The forms of cooperation "are not fixed but exist as a spectrum. An organization acting as a service provider will have a position on this spectrum, which will vary depending on its strategy and objectives for customer relationships." Ref 3.3 C. Correct. "Corporate culture: some organizations have a historical preference for one approach over another. Long-standing cultural bias is difficult to change without compelling reasons." Ref 3.3 D. Incorrect. The level of formality depends on the form of cooperation, which in turn depends on the supplier strategy. The forms of cooperation "are not fixed but exist as a spectrum. An organization acting as a service provider will have a position on this spectrum, which will vary depending on its strategy and objectives for customer relationships." Ref 3.3
28	C	6.2.f	A. Incorrect. Change is "The addition, modification, or removal of anything that could have a direct or indirect effect on services." Ref 5.2.4 B. Incorrect. An event is "Any change of state that has significance for the management of a service or other configuration item (CI). Events are typically recognized through notifications created by an IT service, CI, or monitoring tool." Ref 5.2.7 C. Correct. A problem is "a cause, or potential cause, of one or more incidents." Ref 5.2.8 D. Incorrect. An incident is "An unplanned interruption to a service or reduction in the quality of a service." Ref 5.2.5

The ITIL® 4 Foundation Examination

Q	A	Syllabus Ref	Rationale
29	B	6.1.b	A. Incorrect. "The purpose of the continual improvement practice is to align the organization's practices and services with changing business needs through the ongoing improvement of products, services, and practices, or any element involved in the management of products and services." Ref 5.1.2 B. Correct. "The purpose of the relationship management practice is to establish and nurture the links between the organization and its stakeholders at strategic and tactical levels. It includes the identification, analysis, monitoring, and continual improvement of relationships with and between stakeholders." Ref 5.1.9 C. Incorrect. "The purpose of the problem management practice is to reduce the likelihood and impact of incidents by identifying actual and potential causes of incidents, and managing workarounds and known errors." Ref 5.2.8 D. Incorrect. "The purpose of the incident management practice is to minimize the negative impact of incidents by restoring normal service operation as quickly as possible." Ref 5.2.5
30	B	2.1	A. Incorrect. "To support a holistic approach to service management, ITIL defines four dimensions that collectively are critical to the effective and efficient facilitation of value for customers and other stakeholders in the form of products and services." Adopting ITIL to address these four dimensions of ITSM helps to facilitate value but does not help the organization to adapt ITIL guidance to its organization. Ref 3 B. Correct. The guiding principles can "guide organizations in their work as they adopt a service management approach and adapt ITIL guidance to their own specific needs and circumstances." Ref 4.3 C. Incorrect. "Service value chain: A set of interconnected activities that an organization performs to deliver a valuable product or service to its consumers and to facilitate value realization." Adopting a service value chain helps to facilitate value but does not help the organization to adapt ITIL guidance to its organization. Ref 4.1 D. Incorrect. Practices are sets of organizational resources designed for performing work or accomplishing an objective. They do not help the organization to adapt ITIL guidance to its organization. Ref 4.1
31	D	1.2.e	A. Incorrect. An event is: "Any change of state that has significance for the management of a service or other configuration item (CI). Events are typically recognized through notifications created by an IT service, CI, or monitoring tool." Ref 5.2.7 B. Incorrect. Risk is "A possible event that could cause harm or loss, or make it more difficult to achieve objectives." Ref 2.5.3 C. Incorrect. An outcome is "A result for a stakeholder enabled by one or more outputs." Ref 2.5.1 D. Correct. An output is "A tangible or intangible deliverable of an activity". Ref 2.5.1

The ITIL® 4 Foundation Examination

Q	A	Syllabus Ref	Rationale
32	C	7.1.g	A. Incorrect. There would not be fewer metrics gathered, although it would combine and aggregate them to provide clearer information. "The practice requires pragmatic focus on the whole service and not simply its constituent parts; for example, simple individual metrics (such as percentage system availability) should not be taken to represent the whole service." Ref 5.2.15 B. Incorrect. The reason is to reduce reporting of the individual system-based metrics which are not meaningful to the customer. "They should relate to defined outcomes and not simply operational metrics. This can be achieved with balanced bundles of metrics." Ref 5.2.15.1 C. Correct. "They should relate to defined outcomes and not simply operational metrics. This can be achieved with balanced bundles of metrics." Ref 5.2.15.1 D. Incorrect. This does not affect the mechanism for metric collection. "The practice requires pragmatic focus on the whole service and not simply its constituent parts; for example, simple individual metrics (such as percentage system availability) should not be taken to represent the whole service." Ref 5.2.15
33	C	7.1.c	A. Incorrect. "Modern IT service management tools can provide automated matching of incidents to other incidents, problems or known errors," but this is not dependent on the incident priority, which is used to ensure that incidents with the highest business impact are resolved first. Ref 5.2.5 B. Incorrect. "More complex incidents will usually be escalated to a support team for resolution. Typically, the routing is based on the incident category, which should help to identify the correct team." Ref 5.2.5 C. Correct. "Incidents are prioritized based on an agreed classification to ensure that incidents with the highest business impact are resolved first." Ref 5.2.5 D. Incorrect. "Effective incident management often requires a high level of collaboration within and between teams." However, this is not dependent on the incident priority, which is used to "ensure that incidents with the highest business impact are resolved first". Ref 5.2.5
34	B	6.1.d	A. Incorrect. "The purpose of the relationship management practice is to establish and nurture the links between the organization and its stakeholders at strategic and tactical levels." Ref 5.1.9 B. Correct. "The purpose of the IT asset management practice is to plan and manage the full lifecycle of all IT assets, to help the organization: maximize value, control costs, manage risks." Ref 5.2.6 C. Incorrect. "The purpose of the release management practice is to make new and changed services and features available for use." Ref 5.2.9 D. Incorrect. "The purpose of the service desk practice is to capture demand for incident resolution and service requests." Ref 5.2.14

The ITIL® 4 Foundation Examination

Q	A	Syllabus Ref	Rationale
35	A	7.1.d	A. Correct. "Problem identification activities identify and log problems. These include:... detection of duplicate and recurring issues by users, service desk, and technical support staff." Ref 5.2.8 B. Incorrect. Identifying the correct team for escalating an incident is based on incident category, not recurring incidents. "More complex incidents will usually be escalated to a support team for resolution. Typically, the routing is based on the incident category, which should help to identify the correct team." Ref 5.2.5 C. Incorrect. "The purpose of the service request management practice is to support the agreed quality of a service by handling all pre-defined, user-initiated service requests in an effective and user-friendly manner." Detection of recurring issues by the service desk is not required to do this. Ref 5.2.16 D. Incorrect. "The person or group who authorizes a change is known as a change authority. It is essential that the correct change authority is assigned to each type of change to ensure that change enablement is both efficient and effective." This assignment is based on the type of change, and detection of recurring issues by the service desk is not required to do this. Ref 5.2.4
36	D	5.2.a	A. Incorrect. "The purpose of the improve value chain activity is to ensure continual improvement of products, services, and practices across all value chain activities and the four dimensions of service management." Ref 4.5.2 B. Incorrect. "The purpose of the engage value chain activity is to provide a good understanding of stakeholder needs, transparency, and continual engagement and good relationships with all stakeholders." Ref 4.5.3 C. Incorrect. "The purpose of the obtain/build value chain activity is to ensure that service components are available when and where they are needed, and meet agreed specifications." Ref 4.5.5 D. Correct. "The purpose of the plan value chain activity is to ensure a shared understanding of the vision, current status, and improvement direction for all four dimensions and all products and services across the organization." Ref 4.5.1

The ITIL® 4 Foundation Examination

Q	A	Syllabus Ref	Rationale
37	D	2.2.a	A. Incorrect. The emphasis of this principle is on how to approach activities: "Always use the minimum number of steps to accomplish an objective. Outcome-based thinking should be used to produce practical solutions that deliver valuable outcomes." Ref 4.3.6 B. Incorrect. This principle is focused on increased effectiveness and efficiency. "Organizations must maximize the value of the work carried out by their human and technical resources." Ref 4.3.7 C. Incorrect. This shows how to approach making changes. "Resist the temptation to do everything at once. Even huge initiatives must be accomplished iteratively. By organizing work into smaller, manageable sections that can be executed and completed in a timely manner, the focus on each effort will be sharper and easier to maintain." Ref 4.3.3 D. Correct. "This section is mostly focused on the creation of value for service consumers... This value may come in various forms, such as revenue, customer loyalty, lower cost, or growth opportunities." Ref 4.3.1
38	B	7.1.g	A. Incorrect. "Service desks provide a clear path for users to report issues, queries, and requests, and have them acknowledged, classified, owned, and actioned." Ref 5.2.14 B. Correct. "Service level management provides the end-to-end visibility of the organization's services. To achieve this, service level management:... captures and reports on service issues, including performance against defined service levels." Ref 5.2.14 C. Incorrect. "A request from a user or a user's authorized representative that initiates a service action which has been agreed as a normal part of service delivery." Ref 5.2.15 D. Incorrect. "Service configuration management collects and manages information about a wide variety of CIs, typically including hardware, software, networks, buildings, people, suppliers, and documentation." Ref 5.2.11

The ITIL® 4 Foundation Examination

Q	A	Syllabus Ref	Rationale
39	C	7.1.b	A. Incorrect. Emergency changes "are changes that must be implemented as soon as possible; for example, to resolve an incident or implement a security patch." The implementation of a planned new release of a software application does not fall into this category and would be planned and implemented as a normal change. Ref 5.2.4 B. Incorrect. Emergency changes "are changes that must be implemented as soon as possible; for example, to resolve an incident or implement a security patch." A low-risk computer upgrade implemented as a service request does not fall into this category. Using a service request implies that this is a standard change, as standard changes "are often initiated as service requests." Ref 5.2.4 C. Correct. Emergency changes are "Changes that must be implemented as soon as possible; for example, to resolve an incident or implement a security patch." Ref 5.2.4 D. Incorrect. Emergency changes "must be implemented as soon as possible; for example, to resolve an incident or implement a security patch. Emergency changes are not typically included in a change schedule, and the process for assessment and authorization is expedited to ensure they can be implemented quickly." A scheduled major hardware and software implementation does not fall into this category and would be planned and implemented as a normal change. Ref 5.2.4
40	B	2.2.b	A. Incorrect. The guiding principle 'focus on value' advises "All activities conducted by the organization should link back, directly or indirectly, to value for itself, its customers, and other stakeholders." This is not the main concern of the guiding principle 'start where you are'. Ref 4.3.1 B. Correct. The guiding principle 'start where you are' advises "Having a proper understanding of the current state of services and methods is important to selecting which elements to re-use, alter, or build upon." Ref 4.3.2.3 C. Incorrect. The focus of the guiding principle 'collaborate and promote visibility' is on involving the right stakeholders and communicating with them. "When initiatives involve the right people in the correct roles, efforts benefit from better buy-in, more relevance (because better information is available for decision-making) and increased likelihood of long-term success". This is not the main concern of the guiding principle 'start where you are'. Ref 4.3.4 D. Incorrect. The main concern of the guiding principle 'progress iteratively with feedback' is breaking initiatives into smaller parts. "By organizing work into smaller, manageable sections that can be executed and completed in a timely manner, the focus on each effort will be sharper and easier to maintain." This is not the main concern of the guiding principle 'start where you are'. Ref 4.3.3

Updates to ITIL 4 Foundation Syllabus – January 2019

The following table outlines changes that have been made to the ITIL 4 Foundation Syllabus to reflect feedback provided from the ATO and trainer community during Train-the-Trainer events.

For awareness, with the reduction in the scope of Assessment Criteria 5.2 as outlined below, the number of questions in this section has been reduced by two. These questions have been reallocated to sections 7.1 and 2.2 to slightly increase the focus on the Guiding Principles and key practices.

In addition, the references in assessment criteria 2.2 & 7.1g have been updated to reflect minor structural changes in the guidance. No content has been removed or added as a result of this change.

Assessment Criteria affected	Overview of change	Rationale
5.2	'Describe the inputs, outputs and purpose of each value chain activity' has changed to 'Describe the purpose of each value chain activity'.	To enable trainers to focus more on each activity of the Service Value Chain, rather than the list of inputs and outputs.
6.1	The following practices have been removed from scope of this assessment criteria: - Availability Management - Capacity and Performance Management - Service Continuity Management	To enable trainers to apply a more creative, interactive teaching approach to covering other key practices.
6.2	The following term has been removed from examinable scope: - Availability	As we are removing Availability Management from the scope of assessment criteria 6.1, this term is no longer examinable.
7.1	'Explain the following ITIL practices in detail, including how they fit within the service value chain' has changed to 'Explain the following ITIL practices in detail, excluding how they fit within the service value chain'.	The relationship between these practices and how they fit within the service value chain will be explored in greater detail in future publications. In removing this theoretical component from the scope of the Foundation syllabus, we aim to allow trainers more time to deepen candidates understanding of these practices in general by providing more practical guidance on them.

ITIL 4 Foundation Glossary

Term/ Concept	Definition / Explanation
acceptance criteria	A list of minimum requirements that a service or service component must meet for it to be acceptable to key stakeholders.
Agile	An umbrella term for a collection of frameworks and techniques that together enable teams and individuals to work in a way that is typified by collaboration, prioritization, iterative and incremental delivery, and timeboxing. There are several specific methods (or frameworks) that are classed as Agile, such as Scrum, Lean, and Kanban.
Architecture management practice	The practice of providing an understanding of all the different elements that make up an organization and how those elements relate to one another.
asset register	A database or list of assets, capturing key attributes such as ownership and financial value.
availability	The ability of an IT service or other configuration item to perform its agreed function when required.
Availability management practice	The practice of ensuring that services deliver agreed levels of availability to meet the needs of customers and users.
baseline	A report or metric that serves as a starting point against which progress or change can be assessed.
best practice	A way of working that has been proven to be successful by multiple organizations.
big data	The use of very large volumes of structured and unstructured data from a variety of sources to gain new insights.
business analysis practice	The practice of analysing a business or some element of a business, defining its needs and recommending solutions to address these needs and/or solve a business problem, and create value for stakeholders.
business case	A justification for expenditure of organizational resources, providing information about costs, benefits, options, risks, and issues.
business impact analysis (BIA)	A key activity in the practice of service continuity management that identifies vital business functions and their dependencies.
business relationship manager (BRM)	A role responsible for maintaining good relationships with one or more customers.
call	An interaction (e.g. a telephone call) with the service desk. A call could result in an incident or a service request being logged.
call/contact centre	An organization or business unit that handles large numbers of incoming and outgoing calls and other interactions.
capability	The ability of an organization, person, process, application, configuration item, or IT service to carry out an activity.
capacity and performance management practice	The practice of ensuring that services achieve agreed and expected performance levels, satisfying current and future demand in a costeffective way.
capacity planning	The activity of creating a plan that manages resources to meet demand for services.
Change	The addition, modification, or removal of anything that could have a direct or indirect effect on services.
change authority	A person or group responsible for authorizing a change.

ITIL 4 Foundation Glossary

change control practice	The practice of ensuring that risks are properly assessed, authorizing changes to proceed and managing a change schedule in order to maximize the number of successful IT changes.
change model	A repeatable approach to the management of a particular type of change.
change schedule	A calendar that shows planned and historical changes.
Charging	The activity that assigns a price for services.
cloud computing	A model for enabling on-demand network access to a shared pool of configurable computing resources that can be rapidly provided with minimal management effort or provider interaction.
compliance	The act of ensuring that a standard or set of guidelines is followed, or that proper, consistent accounting or other practices are being employed.
confidentiality	A security objective that ensures information is not made available or disclosed to unauthorized entities.
configuration	An arrangement of configuration items (CIs) or other resources that work together to deliver a product or service. Can also be used to describe the parameter settings for one or more CIs.
configuration item (CI)	Any component that needs to be managed in order to deliver an IT service.
Configuration management database (CMDB)	A database used to store configuration records throughout their lifecycle. The CMDB also maintains the relationships between configuration records.
Configuration management system (CMS)	A set of tools, data, and information that is used to support service configuration management.
configuration record	A record containing the details of a configuration item (CI). Each configuration record documents the lifecycle of a single CI. Configuration records are stored in a configuration management database.
continual improvement practice	The practice of aligning an organization's practices and services with changing business needs through the ongoing identification and improvement of all elements involved in the effective management of products and services.
Continuous integration/continuous delivery (CI/CD)	An integrated set of practices and tools used to merge developers' code, build and test the resulting software, and package it so that it is ready for deployment.
Control	The means of managing a risk, ensuring that a business objective is achieved, or that a process is followed.
Cost	The amount of money spent on a specific activity or resource.
cost centre	A business unit or project to which costs are assigned.
critical success factor (CSF)	A necessary precondition for the achievement of intended results.
Culture	A set of values that is shared by a group of people, including expectations about how people should behave, ideas, beliefs, and practices.
Customer	A person who defines the requirements for a service and takes responsibility for the outcomes of service consumption.
customer experience (CX)	The sum of functional and emotional interactions with a service and service provider as perceived by a service consumer.
Dashboard	A real-time graphical representation of data.

ITIL 4 Foundation Glossary

deliver and support	The value chain activity that ensures services are delivered and supported according to agreed specifications and stakeholders' expectations.
Demand	Input to the service value system based on opportunities and needs from internal and external stakeholders.
Deployment	The movement of any service component into any environment.
Deployment management practice	The practice of moving new or changed hardware, software, documentation, processes, or any other service component to live environments.
design and transition	The value chain activity that ensures products and services continually meet stakeholder expectations for quality, costs, and time to market.
design thinking	A practical and human-centred approach used by product and service designers to solve complex problems and find practical and creative solutions that meet the needs of an organization and its customers.
Development environment	An environment used to create or modify IT services or applications.
DevOps	An organizational culture that aims to improve the flow of value to customers. DevOps focuses on culture, automation, Lean, measurement, and sharing (CALMS).
digital transformation	The evolution of traditional business models to meet the needs of highly empowered customers, with technology playing an enabling role.
disaster recovery plans	A set of clearly defined plans related to how an organization will recover from a disaster as well as return to a pre-disaster condition, considering the four dimensions of service management.
Driver	Something that influences strategy, objectives, or requirements.
Effectiveness	A measure of whether the objectives of a practice, service or activity have been achieved.
Efficiency	A measure of whether the right amount of resources have been used by a practice, service, or activity.
emergency change	A change that must be introduced as soon as possible.
Engage	The value chain activity that provides a good understanding of stakeholder needs, transparency, continual engagement, and good relationships with all stakeholders.
Environment	A subset of the IT infrastructure that is used for a particular purpose, for example a live environment or test environment. Can also mean the external conditions that influence or affect something.
Error	A flaw or vulnerability that may cause incidents.
error control	Problem management activities used to manage known errors.
Escalation	The act of sharing awareness or transferring ownership of an issue or work item.
Event	Any change of state that has significance for the management of a service or other configuration item.
external customer	A customer who works for an organization other than the service provider.
Failure	A loss of ability to operate to specification, or to deliver the required output or outcome.
feedback loop	A technique whereby the outputs of one part of a system are used as inputs to the same part of the system.
four dimensions of service management	The four perspectives that are critical to the effective and efficient facilitation of value for customers and other stakeholders in the form of products and services.

ITIL 4 Foundation Glossary

governance	The means by which an organization is directed and controlled.
Identity	A unique name that is used to identify and grant system access rights to a user, person, or role.
Improve	The value chain activity that ensures continual improvement of products, services, and practices across all value chain activities and the four dimensions of service management.
Incident	An unplanned interruption to a service or reduction in the quality of a service.
incident management	The practice of minimizing the negative impact of incidents by restoring normal service operation as quickly as possible.
information and technology	One of the four dimensions of service management. It includes the information and knowledge used to deliver services, and the information and technologies used to manage all aspects of the service value system.
information security management practice	The practice of protecting an organization by understanding and managing risks to the confidentiality, integrity, and availability of information.
information security policy	The policy that governs an organization's approach to information security management.
infrastructure and platform management practice	The practice of overseeing the infrastructure and platforms used by an organization. This enables the monitoring of technology solutions available, including solutions from third parties.
Integrity	A security objective that ensures information is only modified by authorized personnel and activities.
internal customer	A customer who works for the same organization as the service provider.
Internet of Things	The interconnection of devices via the internet that were not traditionally thought of as IT assets, but now include embedded computing capability and network connectivity.
IT asset	Any valuable component that can contribute to the delivery of an IT product or service.
IT asset management practice	The practice of planning and managing the full lifecycle of all IT assets.
IT infrastructure	All of the hardware, software, networks, and facilities that are required to develop, test, deliver, monitor, manage, and support IT services.
IT service	A service based on the use of information technology.
ITIL	Best-practice guidance for IT service management.
ITIL guiding principles	Recommendations that can guide an organization in all circumstances, regardless of changes in its goals, strategies, type of work, or management structure.
ITIL service value chain	An operating model for service providers that covers all the key activities required to effectively manage products and services.
Kanban	A method for visualizing work, identifying potential blockages and resource conflicts, and managing work in progress.
key performance indicator (KPI)	An important metric used to evaluate the success in meeting an objective.
Knowledge management practice	The practice of maintaining and improving the effective, efficient, and convenient use of information and knowledge across an organization.
known error	A problem that has been analysed but has not been resolved.

ITIL 4 Foundation Glossary

Lean	An approach that focuses on improving workflows by maximizing value through the elimination of waste.
Lifecycle	The full set of stages, transitions, and associated statuses in the life of a service, product, practice, or other entity.
Live	Refers to a service or other configuration item operating in the live environment.
live environment	A controlled environment used in the delivery of IT services to service consumers.
Maintainability	The ease with which a service or other entity can be repaired or modified.
major incident	An incident with significant business impact, requiring an immediate coordinated resolution.
management system	Interrelated or interacting elements that establish policy and objectives and enable the achievement of those objectives.
Maturity	A measure of the reliability, efficiency and effectiveness of an organization, practice, or process.
mean time between failures (MTBF)	A metric of how frequently a service or other configuration item fails.
mean time to restore service (MTRS)	A metric of how quickly a service is restored after a failure.
measurement and reporting	The practice of supporting good decision-making and continual improvement by decreasing levels of uncertainty.
Metric	A measurement or calculation that is monitored or reported for management and improvement.
minimum viable product (MVP)	A product with just enough features to satisfy early customers, and to provide feedback for future product development.
mission statement	A short but complete description of the overall purpose and intentions of an organization. It states what is to be achieved, but not how this should be done.
Model	A representation of a system, practice, process, service, or other entity that is used to understand and predict its behaviour and relationships.
Modelling	The activity of creating, maintaining, and utilizing models.
Monitoring	Repeated observation of a system, practice, process, service, or other entity to detect events and to ensure that the current status is known.
monitoring and event management practice	The practice of systematically observing services and service components, and recording and reporting selected changes of state identified as events.
obtain/build	The value chain activity that ensures service components are available when and where they are needed, and that they meet agreed specifications.
Operation	The routine running and management of an activity, product, service, or other configuration item.
operational technology	The hardware and software solutions that detect or cause changes in physical processes through direct monitoring and/or control of physical devices such as valves, pumps, etc.
organization	A person or a group of people that has its own functions with responsibilities, authorities, and relationships to achieve its objectives.
organizational change management practice	The practice of ensuring that changes in an organization are smoothly and successfully implemented and that lasting benefits are achieved by managing the human aspects of the changes.

ITIL 4 Foundation Glossary

organizational resilience	The ability of an organization to anticipate, prepare for, respond to, and adapt to unplanned external influences.
organizational velocity	The speed, effectiveness, and efficiency with which an organization operates. Organizational velocity influences time to market, quality, safety, costs, and risks.
organizations and people	One of the four dimensions of service management. It ensures that the way an organization is structured and managed, as well as its roles, responsibilities, and systems of authority and communication, is well defined and supports its overall strategy and operating model.
Outcome	A result for a stakeholder enabled by one or more outputs.
Output	A tangible or intangible deliverable of an activity.
Outsourcing	The process of having external suppliers provide products and services that were previously provided internally.
partners and suppliers	One of the four dimensions of service management. It encompasses the relationships an organization has with other organizations that are involved in the design, development, deployment, delivery, support, and/or continual improvement of services.
Partnership	A relationship between two organizations that involves working closely together to achieve common goals and objectives.
Performance	A measure of what is achieved or delivered by a system, person, team, practice, or service.
Pilot	A test implementation of a service with a limited scope in a live environment.
Plan	The value chain activity that ensures a shared understanding of the vision, current status, and improvement direction for all four dimensions and all products and services across an organization.
Policy	Formally documented management expectations and intentions, used to direct decisions and activities.
portfolio management practice	The practice of ensuring that an organization has the right mix of programmes, projects, products, and services to execute its strategy within its funding and resource constraints.
post-implementation review (PIR)	A review after the implementation of a change, to evaluate success and identify opportunities for improvement.
Practice	A set of organizational resources designed for performing work or accomplishing an objective.
Problem	A cause, or potential cause, of one or more incidents.
problem management practice	The practice of reducing the likelihood and impact of incidents by identifying actual and potential causes of incidents, and managing workarounds and known errors.
Procedure	A documented way to carry out an activity or a process.
Process	A set of interrelated or interacting activities that transform inputs into outputs. A process takes one or more defined inputs and turns them into defined outputs. Processes define the sequence of actions and their dependencies.
Product	A configuration of an organization's resources designed to offer value for a consumer.
production environment	See live environment.

ITIL 4 Foundation Glossary

Programme	A set of related projects and activities, and an organization structure created to direct and oversee them.
Project	A temporary structure that is created for the purpose of delivering one or more outputs (or products) according to an agreed business case.
project management practice	The practice of ensuring that all an organization's projects are successfully delivered.
quick win	An improvement that is expected to provide a return on investment in a short period of time with relatively small cost and effort.
Record	A document stating results achieved and providing evidence of activities performed.
Recovery	The activity of returning a configuration item to normal operation after a failure.
recovery point objective (RPO)	The point to which information used by an activity must be restored to enable the activity to operate on resumption.
recovery time objective (RTO)	The maximum acceptable period of time following a service disruption that can elapse before the lack of business functionality severely impacts the organization.
relationship management practice	The practice of establishing and nurturing links between an organization and its stakeholders at strategic and tactical levels.
Release	A version of a service or other configuration item, or a collection of configuration items, that is made available for use.
release management practice	The practice of making new and changed services and featuresavailable for use.
Reliability	The ability of a product, service, or other configuration item to perform its intended function for a specified period of time or number of cycles.
request catalogue	A view of the service catalogue, providing details on service requests for existing and new services, which is made available for the user.
request for change (RFC)	A description of a proposed change used to initiate change control.
Resolution	The action of solving an incident or problem.
Resource	A person, or other entity, that is required for the execution of an activity or the achievement of an objective.
Retire	The act of permanently withdrawing a product, service, or other configuration item from use.
Risk	A possible event that could cause harm or loss, or make it more difficult to achieve objectives. Can also be defined as uncertainty of outcome, and can be used in the context of measuring the probability of positive outcomes as well as negative outcomes.
risk assessment	An activity to identify, analyse, and evaluate risks.
risk management practice	The practice of ensuring that an organization understands and effectively handles risks.
Service	A means of enabling value co-creation by facilitating outcomes that customers want to achieve, without the customer having to manage specific costs and risks.
service architecture	A view of all the services provided by an organization. It includes interactions between the services, and service models that describe the structure and dynamics of each service.

ITIL 4 Foundation Glossary

service catalogue	Structured information about all the services and service offerings of a service provider, relevant for a specific target audience.
service catalogue management practice	The practice of providing a single source of consistent information on all services and service offerings, and ensuring that it is available to the relevant audience.
service configuration management practice	The practice of ensuring that accurate and reliable information about the configuration of services, and the configuration items that support them, is available when and where needed.
service consumption	Activities performed by an organization to consume services. It includes the management of the consumer's resources needed to use the service, service actions performed by users, and the receiving (acquiring) of goods (if required).
service continuity management practice	The practice of ensuring that service availability and performance are maintained at a sufficient level in the event of a disaster.
service design practice	The practice of designing products and services that are fit for purpose, fit for use, and that can be delivered by the organization and its ecosystem.
service desk	The point of communication between the service provider and all its users.
service desk practice	The practice of capturing demand for incident resolution and service requests.
service financial management practice	The practice of supporting an organization's strategies and plans for service management by ensuring that the organization's financial resources and investments are being used effectively.
service level	A set of measurable parameters defining expected or achieved service quality.
service level agreement (SLA)	A documented agreement between a service provider and a customer that identifies both services required and the expected level of service.
service level management practice	The practice of setting clear business-based targets for service performance so that the delivery of a service can be properly assessed, monitored, and managed against these targets.
service management	A set of specialized organizational capabilities for enabling value for customers in the form of services.
service offering	A description of one or more services, designed to address the needs of a target consumer group. A service offering may include goods, access to resources, and service actions.
service owner	A role that is accountable for the delivery of a specific service.
service portfolio	A complete set of products and services that are managed throughout their lifecycles by an organization.
service provider	A role performed by an organization in a service relationship to provide services to consumers.
service provision	Activities performed by an organization to provide services. It includes management of resources, configured to deliver the service, access to these resources for users, fulfilment of the agreed service actions, service performance management, and continual improvement. It may also include the supply of goods.
service relationship	A cooperation between a service provider and service consumer. Service relationships include service provision, service consumption, and service relationship management.
service relationship management	Joint activities performed by a service provider and a service consumer to ensure continual value co-creation based on agreed and available service offerings.

ITIL 4 Foundation Glossary

Term	Definition
service request	A request from a user or a user's authorized representative that initiates a service action which has been agreed as a normal part of service delivery.
service request management practice	The practice of supporting the agreed quality of a service by handling all pre-defined, user-initiated service requests in an effective and userfriendly manner.
service validation and testing practice	The practice of ensuring that new or changed products and services meet defined requirements.
service value system (SVS)	A model representing how all the components and activities of an organization work together to facilitate value creation.
software development and management practice	The practice of ensuring that applications meet stakeholder needs in terms of functionality, reliability, maintainability, compliance, and auditability.
sourcing	The activity of planning and obtaining resources from a particular source type, which could be internal or external, centralized or distributed, and open or proprietary.
specification	A documented description of the properties of a product, service, or other configuration item.
sponsor	A person who authorizes budget for service consumption. Can also be used to describe an organization or individual that provides financial or other support for an initiative.
stakeholder	A person or organization that has an interest or involvement in an organization, product, service, practice, or other entity.
standard	A document, established by consensus and approved by a recognized body, that provides for common and repeated use, mandatory requirements, guidelines, or characteristics for its subject.
standard change	A low-risk, pre-authorized change that is well understood and fully documented, and which can be implemented without needing additional authorization.
status	A description of the specific states an entity can have at a given time.
strategy management practice	The practice of formulating the goals of an organization and adopting the courses of action and allocation of resources necessary for achieving those goals.
supplier	A stakeholder responsible for providing services that are used by an organization.
supplier management practice	The practice of ensuring that an organization's suppliers and their performance levels are managed appropriately to support the provision of seamless quality products and services.
support team	A team with the responsibility to maintain normal operations, address users' requests, and resolve incidents and problems related to specified products, services, or other configuration items.
system	A combination of interacting elements organized and maintained to achieve one or more stated purposes.
systems thinking	A holistic approach to analysis that focuses on the way that a system's constituent parts work, interrelate, and interact over time, and within the context of other systems.
technical debt	The total rework backlog accumulated by choosing workarounds instead of system solutions that would take longer.
test environment	A controlled environment established to test products, services, and other configuration items.

ITIL 4 Foundation Glossary

third party	A stakeholder external to an organization.
throughput	A measure of the amount of work performed by a product, service, or other system over a given period of time.
transaction	A unit of work consisting of an exchange between two or more participants or systems.
use case	A technique using realistic practical scenarios to define functional requirements and to design tests.
user	A person who uses services.
utility	The functionality offered by a product or service to meet a particular need.
utility requirements	Functional requirements which have been defined by the customer and are unique to a specific product.
validation	Confirmation that the system, product, service, or other entity meets the agreed specification.
value	The perceived benefits, usefulness, and importance of something.
value stream	A series of steps an organization undertakes to create and deliver products and services to consumers.
value streams and processes	One of the four dimensions of service management. It defines the activities, workflows, controls, and procedures needed to achieve the agreed objectives.
vision	A defined aspiration of what an organization would like to become in the future.
warranty	Assurance that a product or service will meet agreed requirements.
warranty requirements	Typically non-functional requirements captured as inputs from key stakeholders and other practices.
waterfall method	A development approach that is linear and sequential with distinct objectives for each phase of development.
work instruction	A detailed description to be followed in order to perform an activity.
workaround	A solution that reduces or eliminates the impact of an incident or problem for which a full resolution is not yet available. Some workarounds reduce the likelihood of incidents.
workforce and talent management practice	The practice of ensuring that an organization has the right people with the appropriate skills and knowledge and in the correct roles to support its business objectives.